Women Inspiring Nations
Volume 3
I'm Still Standing

Presented by
Dr. Cheryl Wood

ISBN: 978-1-7923-5526-4
Kindle ISBN: 978-1-7923-5527-1

INTRODUCTION
Presented by Dr. Cheryl Wood
Visionary of Women Inspiring Nations Series
12x Best-Selling Author | International Empowerment Speaker | TEDx Speaker | Women's Empowerment Champion

Every woman has a story and every woman's story deserves to be told! If you ever want to know a woman's heart, spirit, and journey just sit her down and listen. The *Women Inspiring Nations* series is designed to give you an exclusive opportunity to "listen" to the most personal and impactful stories of women that you'll ever read. *Women Inspiring Nations* is a powerful platform designed for women from all backgrounds and walks of life, with a variety of unique experiences and perspectives, to courageously share their stories as victors not victims. And *Women Inspiring Nations Volume 3: I'm Still Standing* does not disappoint. I celebrate each of the co-authors who said YES to sharing their stories as a part of this project. There is unparalleled power in sharing your story!

The *Women Inspiring Nations* series is dedicated to women by women: may it remind you that you are destined for greatness and inspire you to claim your personal power over every challenge you might face in order to become the best version of yourself. This powerful collection of empowering personal stories demonstrates the bold, tenacious, and resilient spirit of women globally. Each of the co-authors of *Women Inspiring Nations Volume 3* boldly shares her "I'm Still Standing" story which encompasses her unique struggles and how she overcame her challenges to find ultimate success. *Women Inspiring Nations*

Volume 3 will propel you to embrace the belief that no struggle can hold you back from fulfilling your destiny unless you allow it to. Remember, you have a unique fingerprint that is meant to make a lasting impression on the world, and your story is a big part of that lasting impression!

I began sharing my personal life story in 2009 and ultimately discovered that it is much more painful to keep your story comfortably tucked inside of you than it is to intentionally expose your raw, authentic truth without guilt or shame. Author and Poet Maya Angelou herself penned these words of truth, "There is no greater agony than bearing an untold story inside of you." As a young girl who was raised in poverty in a housing project in Baltimore, Maryland, I never imagined a time such as this where I would be able to look back and see how drastically God has elevated me in my life. I take that elevation as a personal responsibility to share how God has brought me through some of the most difficult challenges I've experienced in my life, including all types of trauma and loss. As I have bounced back from every challenge, I have become more aware and confident about who I am and whose I am, and more conscious of the need to share my experiences. Most importantly, I have learned this fact about every woman's story, "Your story is *about* you but it's not *for* you!"

Every time a woman shares her story, not only does she create freedom for herself, but she also creates freedom for other women who can see themselves in her story and are inspired to endure. And that's what makes our lives and our experiences really matter … being able to share our unique experiences, knowledge, lessons learned, and even the unforeseen, sometimes messy, parts of our lives so that someone else is inspired enough to persevere through their own struggle, learn their own lessons, overcome their own trauma, triumph over their own setbacks, and/or develop more hope and belief in their own dreams.

As you take this deep dive into *Women Inspiring Nations Volume 3*, you will experience a range of emotions. Each story contains its own set of challenges, discouragement, grief, courage, hope, belief, and triumph. Ultimately, you will see that no matter how successful or accomplished a woman is, she does not arrive there without overcoming struggle. It is my hope that you will read this book and feel more equipped, more empowered, and more inspired than ever before to keep pressing through your own journey without giving up, and to reach back and share your story so that you too can inspire nations. And, most importantly, to remember that just as each of the co-authors is still standing… you can do the same!

Dr. Cheryl Wood
Visionary of Women Inspiring Nations
www.cherylempowers.com
EMAIL: info@cherylwoodempowers.com
SOCIAL MEDIA: @CherylEmpowers

Overcoming Death, Loss, and Tragedy
By Patricia Barnes

Death, loss, and tragedy are sad realities of life that sometimes lead to anxiety, depression, and suicidal thoughts. Learning healthy coping mechanisms and talking about your pain can aid in healing. We ALL have the power to endure and overcome hardships through Jesus Christ. Let me share how I overcame depression and sadness after the person loved the most transitioned to heaven.

On May 4, 2020, my life changed forever. A piece of my heart now resides in heaven. My Grandma V always had my back. She was my best friend and support system! As write this on September 20, 2020, my eyes are filled with tears thinking about the day. I had to pause to allow my tears to fall down my face like raindrops because it's a healthy part of healing. Denying yourself permission to cry prolongs the grieving process. All my life, I dreaded the day I would have to say goodbye to Grandma and never wanted to be the one to find her dead. Not only did I find her dead, but I also took care of her on hospice.

Flashback to when I had a conversation with Grandma. After months of her body fighting to stay alive in the hospital, one minute doing better then the next minute back in the intensive care unit.

"Grandma, the time has come. Something we never wanted to talk about, but I need to know how to honor your wishes if your heart stops beating and your lungs struggle for air. What do you want me to do?" I asked.

She responded, "Let me go."

Even though I said, "Okay," I was thinking to myself that I would fight for her since she doesn't have the strength to fight for herself. I prayed and fasted more.

At this point, Grandma was going back to the intensive care unit for the fifth time. This time I couldn't be there due to the coronavirus, so I called her.

"Hi, Grandma."

"Patricia," she responded.

"Yes?"

Grandma said, "I have two requests."

"Sure! Whatever you want, Grandma," I responded enthusiastically.

Grandma shared, "I want to die at home and eat a hot dog from 7-Eleven with Spaghettios".

"Okay, Grandma," I replied

The grieving stage of acceptance began that day. Once Grandma was home on hospice, I started to wonder if I could handle watching as her body began to decline? My dad and I were her caretakers. We have strong personalities and, at times, clashed because it seemed we were competing over who loved her more and could do a better job taking care of her. Later, I apologized, knowing I was nitpicking because I believed only I could do the job properly and thoroughly, especially because I'm the registered nurse, not dad! Eventually, we worked as a team, respected the qualities each person brought to the table, and more importantly, created a peaceful environment for Grandma.

My prayer changed from healing her on Earth to Lord, I can never let her go but don't want her to suffer, so may your will be done. Grandma took her last breath that day. My prayers and fasting to heal her on Earth only prolonged her agony. I laid in bed with her for 7-8 hours, waiting for the funeral home to pick her up. As time passed, her body became cold. I knew I would never get this moment again. No more late-night crawling in her bed to talk and eventually falling asleep when my heart was heavy. As the funeral home put her in a body bag, I became emotionally triggered because it was inhumane. I thought a stretcher would be more decent. Looking at the body bag, I cried out loud, "God, what am I supposed to do now?" 2020 was supposed to be my year, but how can 2020 be my year losing the person I loved most on earth? Who will I call when I need encouragement? Who will I spend holidays with? Who will love me genuinely without wanting something from me? Who am I going to lean on? Then the Holy Spirit said to depend on Him! You have never been alone, and you won't start now!

I was in the depression stage of grief as I took care of Grandma, and after she passed. I was going to the liquor store a couple times a week drinking 1.5L of wine. Some days I drank wine straight out the bottle although, I never aimed to get drunk. I didn't feel drunk, but maybe my body was numb in disbelief as Grandma was dying and now dead. I kept telling myself that Grandma was dead to move from the denial because denial will delay healing so repeatedly told myself Grandma is dead, and she's not coming back! I wanted to stop this destructive behavior before it became an addiction. The Holy Spirit convicted me with a thought, "this is how people become addicted to drugs and alcohol."

I stopped thinking addiction can't happen to me, or it's just wine, and attempted to slow down. As the days passed, sadness crept up, and I cried to God to give me the strength to live on without Grandma. God reminded me of everything He placed inside me before Grandma's death. God reminded me that I AM an overcomer, Jesus is my strength when I am weak, and He has brought me through the darkest times of my life, such as an abortion and miscarriage. In my high school yearbook, I said God was my best friend. Decades later, he has been. Now I have two best friends that reside in heaven. He is still with me, and so is Grandma in spirit! By trusting God through my pain and sorrow, He has reminded me that Earth is not our home; heaven is. We all must die in the flesh to go back to dust and bones.

Can I encourage you?

Get out of bed, dress up, and go to work, even if you have tears in your eyes and aches in your heart. Together we will get through this! Instead of focusing on the loss, become whole again with joy and happiness! We have to live on as our loved ones would want us to! Don't stop pursuing your dreams. Make your loved ones proud from above. Every accomplishment and celebration will be in loving memory of them! Smile and laugh at the memories created with loved ones. We can uplift each other knowing two things:

1. The Lord is close to the brokenhearted and saves those who are crushed in spirit.- Psalm 34:18 NIV

2. He will wipe every tear from their eyes. There will be no more death or mourning or crying or pain for the old order of things has passed away. -Revelation 21:4 NIV

I know this to be true because Grandma endured many hard and sad times. I witnessed her excitement, knowing her suffering on Earth was ending, and she was preparing for eternal life. She told me a couple of days before she departed earth, with a smile on her face and undeniable joy in her spirit-lifting her arms toward heaven, "I'm going to heaven, it's beautiful, HALLELUJAH!"

Learn healthy coping mechanisms such as joining bereavement groups, seeking therapy, preserving memories (create a memory shadow box and keep traditions going), surrounding yourself with loving people, working out (exercising releases chemicals called endorphins that make you feel happy. If you want to join my free fitness group for inspiration and accountability, go to gopatty.com or @gopattybrand on Facebook and Instagram), focusing on purpose and self-care, doing things that make you happy and uplift your spirit.

Healing takes time! Allow yourself as much time as you need to heal. It's okay to NOT be okay. Cry as much as you need but don't let grief and mourning turn into long-term depression. Let God be your comfort. Jesus loves you so much! Please don't pull away from God but draw closer to Him. He will never forsake or leave you. Not now, not ever! Salvation means you will see your loved ones again in heaven. Forgive people who failed to support you and the deceased! Remember, forgiveness frees you! Forgiving is part of the healing process!

Support others through their loss and grief. Sometimes we don't know what to say or do when someone is dealing with loss. Strategies include reinforcing God's word for comfort, allowing people to talk about the deceased, don't speak ill or negativity of the dead, don't ask questions about how the deceased died, buying food and keepsake gifts, being there to sit in silence, so people know they're not going through this alone, hugging them, helping to clean up, helping to plan the funeral and maintain support after the funeral, praying together, and understanding people grieve differently. Don't take it personally when a grieving person expresses anger towards you. It's misguided anger, a normal part of the grieving stage.

Patricia Barnes

Patricia Barnes is a registered nurse, blogger, motivational speaker, author, and founder of Go Patty LLC. Go Patty is a movement to inspire, motivate, and empower others to overcome pain, fears, and insecurities to become whole (spiritual, personal, interpersonal, mental, emotional, and financial), dream big then take action; and constantly work on personal development and always have fun in between.

Website and blog - gopatty.com
Facebook and Instagram - @gopattybrand
Email - gopattybrand@gmail.com

Show Up, Rebound, and Win
By Nichole M. Bass-Hawk

~The doorway to change is open. You just have to walk through it. ~

Imagine being a little black girl growing up on Detroit's east side with a mother who is addicted to drugs. Imagine being born out of an affair or having an HIV positive father you didn't know existed until you were a teenager. Imagine being diagnosed with an autoimmune disease while being a single mother with little support and stability. Imagine all of this happening before the age of twenty-five.

If the above odds are indicators of a life you're not meant to rebound from, then I have a story for you.

I am a psychotherapist, inspirational speaker, mentor, and phenomenal woman, who was able to overcome the odds that were against me.

I am simply Nichole.

I survived a life of dysfunction, chaos, low self-esteem, isolation, illness, and depression. I was that little black girl from Detroit, resulting from an affair between my married father and my mother.

I didn't know who my father was until I was thirteen years old, mainly because my mother kept me from knowing him. But it wasn't solely her fault because I feel like my dad should have fought harder for me.

It wasn't until I was eighteen years old that we could build a relationship, uninterrupted without any inference from my mother.

My dad would die from HIV when I was twenty-four years old. His death was hard on me; I only had a relationship with him for six years. I loved my dad, and I knew he loved me, even though we had a slightly rocky relationship.

We missed out on so much time together, and I felt resentful toward my parents for allowing this to happen. I felt cheated, hurt, and deprived of having a father. He missed out on so many milestones. He didn't get to see his granddaughter grow up or watch me graduate from college. He didn't get to walk me down the aisle or congratulate me on starting my career. Every time I had an important moment in my life, I would think about how I wished my dad were there. Despite his downfalls, I would do anything to share my life with him.

I'm estranged from my mother. Our relationship was often toxic and volatile due to her always playing the victim. She is narcissistic and is emotionally unavailable to me, which made it hard to build a relationship. She would call me a bitch so much; you would have thought that was my name. It was hard trying to build a meaningful relationship with my mother when she was in the throes of addiction. Ultimately, I decided that it was not healthy for me to continue trying to form that relationship. I no longer allowed myself to feel guilty or controlled and manipulated by her.

Don't get me wrong, I love my mother, and I will continue to pray for her.

Growing up, my childhood was dysfunctional and chaotic. All I wanted was to be loved and supported.

That environment affected my psyche, self-worth, and my state of being. I was a loner and pretty much stayed to myself. If I couldn't trust my mother, how could I trust anyone else? I was embarrassed and ashamed for my friends to find out about her. When you grow up in chaos, chaos is all you know.

I ended up spiraling out of control, never caring about anything, including myself. I was angry. I skipped school, had an attitude, and made bad choices. I was going down the wrong path.

That is until I gave birth to my daughter at the age of twenty.

I was worried about being a mother. I barely had anything to offer my daughter. I didn't know if I would be capable of being compassionate, loving, or patient. I wanted to provide my daughter with stability, love, and a safe home. I wanted her to have the guidance and support I never had.

I did what I could to provide for her, and every decision that I made was for her best interest. I felt like life was giving me a sense of purpose. Having my daughter taught me how to love. I didn't realize I could love someone so much. She became the reason I kept fighting. I finally felt the warmth of hope for the first time. She's the best part of me.

At twenty-three, I started experiencing pain in my body and extreme fatigue. The doctors couldn't figure out what was wrong with me, and it would take them a year before they diagnosed me with Crohn's Disease. Due to my health condition, I started to decline mentally and physically. My doctor had me on Prednisone, a horrible medication that caused me to gain weight and broke my skin out. It affected my mental stability. Yet another obstacle in my life that I had to overcome.

But I had a daughter to raise, so I had to take control of my life.

I realized that to have a better life, I had to stop making excuses (blaming my parents, not feeling worthy, being a single parent, and self-doubt) and start coming up with solutions. It was time to show up and win!

It was a process.

I had to change my mindset and reset my life by getting myself into therapy. Therapy helped me learn a new way of existing and thinking. I started believing in myself. I prayed and asked God to order my steps. One thing about me is if I don't know how to do anything else, I know how to pray.

To keep moving, I enrolled at Wayne State University, where I obtained my bachelor's degree in Sociology and Psychology. I am the first person in my family to graduate from college and have received my master's degree in Mental Health Counseling.

Imagine my surprise when I was asked to speak at commencement. I was the woman who barely graduated from high school, suddenly being asked to speak in public, something I had no experience with. All the self-doubt and internal conversations that I had with myself came back.

I remember thinking, who are you to give a speech? People are going to laugh at you; you don't have anything worthy to say. I kept trying to talk myself out of giving that speech. I wasn't betting on myself; I counted myself out. I heard the voice of God say to me, "who are you to turn down my blessings?"

At that moment, I said, "why not me? I was built to weather the storm."

Every obstacle in my life was preparation for this moment. I had come too far to give up. I made a promise to myself that I would never give up on me ever again. I was the first African American to deliver the commencement speech for the College of Education. I received a standing ovation.

I was proud of myself. That moment would change the trajectory of my life. I knew after that speech; I wanted to inspire others by sharing my gifts and experiences with the world. I thought I knew nothing about winning.

I was wrong.

I have won many times in my life. Being able to provide my daughter with a good life, graduating from college, becoming a psychotherapist - those were my wins. I am in remission with my Crohn's disease. I'm an inspirational public speaker.

I rebounded, and it paid off. I showed up and won!

This is a story for those with insecurities, toxic people in their lives, or negative thoughts. I want you to know that you can and will win!

Here's my advice to you:

1. Dig deep and believe in yourself. Don't underestimate who you are and your capabilities. You matter, and you deserve all the greatness that life has for you.

2. When opportunities present themselves, take a chance. Even if you feel like you're not qualified, you will never know what you're capable of if you give in to your self-doubt.

3. Stand on your faith; it will take you further than you could imagine. God can dream a more abundant dream for you than you can dream for yourself. Faith without works is dead.

4. Do the work; there are no shortcuts. Nothing will come to fruition if you don't put in the work. You get out of life what you put into it.

5. Keep moving. You don't necessarily have to know where you're headed, but you do have to keep going to reach your goals. Life is a process; take it one step at a time.

You were built to weather the storms. **Remember, stars can't shine without darkness.**

Nichole M. Bass-Hawk

Nichole Bass-Hawk is a Prince fanatic, who is always dancing and singing around her living room, driving her family insane. She always says she needs music like she needs air to breathe. You can find Nichole spending her weekends outdoors, exploring the world around her. She is often travelling to new places and immersing herself into different cultures. She's a proud member of the sorority, Sigma Gamma Rho. EE-Yip! She enjoys going to the opera, ballet, and concerts. She loves spending time with her friends and family, especially her daughter, who always keeps her laughing.

Professionally, Nichole is a clinical therapist, mentor, and inspirational speaker. She works exclusively with adolescents and young adults. She is also a reiki practitioner.

To see more of her work, follow her on Twitter and Instagram: @NicholeBassHawk

Losing It ALL While Discovering EVERYTHING!

By Sherae D. Bell

We were amid a separation in 2005, living in different states and my 19-year-old son Antonio was expecting his first child Anashija. My husband Jay was offered an opportunity in California that he felt the Lord was going to bless our marriage and family. With the desire to mend our marriage and the thirst for a fresh start, we began the process of relocating. Jay moved in June, and my daughter Jazmyn and I moved in August. Things were already challenging but knowing that possibly not getting to see my first grandchild be born was heartbreaking.

However, God had already begun to set up what we would later find to be a divine appointment. I reached out to my line sister Stephanie in California, who I hadn't been in contact with for more than ten years. Who would have thought that her job would only be five minutes from my husband's job, especially since California is so big? Yea, only God had a "for such a time as this" moment for the both of us. Esther 4:14b – "And who knows but that you have come to your royal position for such a time as this?" Neither of us were saved when we were in college, well at least I wasn't, but there we were living for God. What a set up for God's purposeful plan. God is always in the details. Psalm 33:11 – "But the plans of the LORD stand firm forever, the purposes of his heart through all generations." Stephanie connected Jay to the men in her church, they prayed for him and our family, and helped him get acclimated to the area. We found a beautiful home in a great neighborhood with fruit trees and a fenced back yard. Now Jazmyn and I were ready to make the full transition to California; all I had to do was call the movers.

We arrived in California in the first week of August with two weeks of clothing. Jay and Jazmyn adapted to California quicker than I did. I was somewhat to myself and distant; I wasn't too keen on building relations because mine and Jay's was lacking. Jazmyn began ninth grade, and I started looking for a job, being selective, not rushing. I came across some temp jobs, but when I called, all were filled except a receptionist's position paying $14.00 per hour. In my last job, I had a receptionist; surely, I wasn't going to be a one. PRIDE! The recruiter said the positions go fast. I politely declined but thought she was just trying to fill her quota. I continued searching, returning with nothing, and then I heard a voice saying, "take that job," just as clear as you can see the words on this paper, but there was no one in the house but me. I ignored it and continued my search, and there it was again, this time louder, "take that job." Those words were on repeat in my mind but with great intensity. It seemed so real but invisible. I accepted the job and started the following Monday. Not only that but earlier that week, God told me to read the book of "Job." I couldn't figure out the purpose and questioned this too. I had never had an encounter like either of these.

It was now 1:00, and the doorbell rang. I got a little excited because I thought it might be my furniture, but I had not received any notifications, so I had no clue who it could be. With caution, I asked, "Who is it?"

A familiar voice answered, "it's me Hon, Jay."

I opened the door quickly and blurted, "What's wrong?" but when I looked in his eyes, I could see disappointment, and out came four dreadful words, "I was let go."

I said, "you joking, right?"

He said, "no, I'm so sorry."

My heart fell to my feet, my demeanor changed, and my body felt so weak, I began to cry in a rage and started yelling. Asking him questions that I knew he didn't have answers to, I slammed the door behind him. The rage and anger intensified. It lasted longer than I care to tell you. I disconnected from some and distanced from others and had a pity party and a who's to blame sleepover. I was making my husband feel bad because I felt he had failed us. What happened to him hearing from God? What was God telling him now? Where was the fresh start for our marriage and family? Where was this great opportunity? This wasn't what I signed up for. I told him that Jazmyn and I were going back to Virginia as soon as our stuff arrived, and he could stay here if he wanted to. When I replay that day in my head, I am ashamed of how I acted and the person I saw. However, that person did not leave immediately; she lingered around. I wanted to call my family, but the embarrassment crept in, and as embarrassment left, God wouldn't let me. I began to grow cold and angrier as the days went by.

I started my new job, but since we only had one car and my husband needed it for interviews, I got up at 4:00 am, was at the bus stop by 5:15 am, then connected to the Bart to meet my third connection to be at work by 8:00 am and did the opposite in the evening to arrive back at 7:30 pm. Three weeks passed, and still no furniture. After much back and forth, we found out that my husband's previous company felt no obligation to pay anything for the move, so our belongings were in SoCal for auctioning due to nonpayment. This devastated me because most of the furniture was antique and handed down to me from my grandmother and my mom. We were living out of suitcases, sleeping on air mattresses, and had furniture that was given to us. Whenever I entered my house, it reminded me of what I had lost and that I gained nothing. With the turmoil that I had created and the anger that I had allowed to manifest in my mind, I began to cry out to God more for understanding. How could my husband miss the signs? He was usually good at hearing from God.

As time went on and everyone was moving forward, I was stuck. I felt like I did not belong there, and I couldn't shake it. My prayer life became intentional, my Bible Study was more focused, and I was now seeking God with a purpose. He was revealing Himself more to me and introducing me to myself. Then one evening, it happened again as I was spending time with the Lord but still being somewhat shady to my husband. I heard that voice again, but this time it was asking me a question. By the way, who does that?

Voice: Why are you mad at your husband?

Me: You know why. How did he miss it?

Voice: And every time you ask, I reveal myself to you more and show you "you." So why are you still mad at your husband?

Me: Because we are still in California.

Voice: Why is it his fault?

But before I could answer. The "Voice" began to play a conversation that I had with the Lord a year prior to us coming to California.

Me: Lord, I need to know you intimately.

Lord: Even if that means losing EVERYTHING?

Me: YES!

Voice: Your husband has endured the loss with grace for your purpose. Your family's needs have been met – that's PROVISION. Your Landlord has not harassed you – that's PROTECTION. You have a core of women loving you where you are and back to a good place – that's DELIVERANCE. And finally, your HUSBAND has continued to love you in your anger – that's UNCONDITIONAL LOVE.

Me: Lord, please forgive me, and thank you for your grace and your mercy.

I fell to my knees and began to cry. THIS was not about my husband, but it was a commitment to me.

When Jay and Jazmyn came home, I apologized, and yet again, they both forgave me and loved me even more. God had ordained this for my growth and my purpose, but I wanted to fight the process of becoming "ME" because becoming "ME" was too uncomfortable. Remember, you only accomplish one thing in your comfort zone, and that's stagnation.

Matthew 1624-26 Then Jesus went to work on his disciples. "Anyone who intends to come with me has to let me lead. You're not in the driver's seat; I am. Don't run from suffering; embrace it. Follow me, and I'll show you how. Self-help is no help at all. Self-sacrifice is the way, my way, to finding yourself, your true self. What kind of deal is it to get everything you want but lose yourself? What could you ever trade your soul for?

Sherae D. Bell

Sherae Bell is a licensed Minister, Author, and Inspirational Speaker. She is the Founder of Affirmed Ministries, Co-Founder of Cut for Christ Ministries, and Owner of Gifts by Journey, LLC. Born and raised in Baltimore City, Sherae attended Baltimore City College HS and Morgan State University. She honorably served her country for six years in the Army Reserves. Sherae has a passion for women and her purpose is to see women delivered and set free from the captivity of their past. She lives out her motto "from a past of shame to a future of deliverance" and has been blessed to speak to women's groups across the country. Sherae is amazed by how God has used trials and tribulations to build a platform for her ministry. Currently, she resides in Leesburg, Virginia with her husband Jay and dog Zori. She has two children, a daughter-in-love, and three grandchildren.

Never Daddy's Princess, But Always The Daughter Of The King
By Kimberly Benham

I thought hard, for many hours on how to start. Beginnings can be as important as how the journey ends. I was 11 the last time I saw my dad alive. It was the day after my birthday, and he had to tell me my grandmother had passed. I wish I would have known then, that would be our last time shared. Back home, life with my stepdad, let's name him Peter, was fine. Peter was a great father figure to me at 11. We went to football games, talked, watched sports, and spent time listening to music. At the age of 12, my father disowned me. Peter was there to hold me and tell me it would be ok. I loved Peter, and I thought I was loved back.

Now at 16, as a sophomore in high school, my life changed forever. Being an A-A/B honor roll student, there was no greater fear than a C. No, I'm wrong there is an F. Any goody-2-shoes, teacher's pets out there? You all will understand my fear. Not only did I have one F, I had two. *Side note: Whoever invented algebra was not under the influence of the Holy Spirit!* So, there I was, holding a letter to my parents from my homeroom teacher. Knowing she was going to call to see if they received the letter. I came home quietly. Peter wasn't home, but my mom was. She had worked the night before and was sleeping. She had four jobs at the time, Peter none. But that's a chapter for another book. I went to the front room to check the answering machine because that's what we did in 1996, we checked the answering

31

machine. We had one missed call. I had done it; I got to the call first. As a goody2shoes, I wouldn't be able to keep this from my mom for long. The conviction would not allow me to have peace. But I had to think of a plan of action to improve the situation first. I went and pressed the play button and heard, "Kimberly, this is your grandfather. Your dad took his life today."

In a single moment, I saw my life and what could never be. I saw myself graduating, getting married. I saw myself become a mother, and in every vision, he wasn't there. I started screaming and ran to my mom. She ran out of her room asking, what was wrong. "He's dead! They said he was dead. My dad is dead!" After calling my grandfather back, we found out my dad had hung himself. It was really true. My dad had died, and I became completely numb. What do I even say? What do I even try to do? Where could I even go to get away from that pain? I went into myself and hid as much as I could.

We went to Atlanta to say a final goodbye. I thought this would be the hardest thing I would face in my life. I was very wrong, oh, so wrong. Once we were back home and Mom was getting ready for work, I was trying to see if I was going to school. As soon as the front door closed, my bedroom door opened. I turned around and immediately felt a slap across my face. I hit the floor on my hands and knees. Instantly tears were flowing. "What did I do?" I asked Peter. "What happened?"

He squatted down to get closer to my face. That's when I saw the thick belt in his hand. That night I was beaten for the first time by Peter. This went on more and more for the next few years. Always while my mom was at work, she never knew.

One night when I was 19, I felt my life was over. Due to the fights, beatings, and him telling me how ugly and worthless I was, I just wanted to go to sleep and never feel pain again. I started a conversation that saved my life.

"I hate you," I said in my room. "Why are you letting all this happen to me? I'm a good girl. I'm doing everything the way I should. Why do I have to feel this pain?"

And then I heard, "You can't hate something you don't believe in."

"I never said I didn't believe in God; I'm just mad at Him"

"If you believe in Him, do you know what the Bible says about him," the voice asked.

"I know that His word can't come back to Him"

"Yes, His Word will never return to Him void. So, know that He knows you. Know that He loves you. He is aware of your pain. He knows every tear. He said this won't last long. This pain will end soon, so hold on."

The presence of God fell in that room, and I gave my life to Christ. I thank God that He didn't hold that anger against me. He knew me before I was ever born and knew I would say those words. But He started healing my heart. I can't say that I was completely healed that night. But I knew I would never be alone again.

As I write this on the anniversary of my dad's death, I have peace. October 3, 2020, makes 24 years.

At 40, I can say proudly that I am healed! It wasn't easy. And I didn't do this alone. Nothing but God's Grace and Love! You can have deliverance also. God is waiting now to heal you, to comfort you.

Know that painful things happen, but you don't have to stay in it. Please know there is help available.

National Suicide Prevention Lifeline
Hours: Available 24 hours. Languages: English, Spanish - 800-273-8255

Kimberly Benham

Kimberly Benham was born in Atlanta, Georgia, on July 17, 1980. She is the mother of two wonderful, beautiful girls: Andrianna and Briana Renae. Benham is pursuing her bachelor's degree in psychology. With her degree, she hopes to write books with a deeper psychological understanding teaching children to always love themselves and see themselves as God created them. Her first published book is "Kenny the Helper Bee" which can be purchased at www.kennythebee.com or on Amazon.

Please contact me at gracioushoneycombllc@icloud.com for information on the second children's book, "Kenny's Letters to God."

The Domino Effect
By Debra A. Bledsoe

Introduction

Most people understand the domino effect. As kids, we lined up the dominoes in a row, making them all fall by pushing just one. Sometimes, life plays out like the domino effect, with a series of positive or negative events. In my case, it was one negative event after another. Such events almost took my life, but one domino was still standing: the *Dunamis Domino*.

Domino One: Domestic Violence

You don't know where you're going if you don't know where you came from. It's taken me more than three decades to identify the influences that have impacted my life. While some were good, many were bad. It wasn't until later in my life, after having my own family, that I understood the inner workings of my upbringing. The aftermath of growing up in a violent household was that my life went spinning out of control for more than a decade.

My parents fought every week. I cannot recall their good times because many of my days, evenings, and weekends were filled with violence and bloodshed. Police visits to our home became routine, yet they never took my dad to jail. Domestic violence laws were not enforced then as they are today. Had they been enforced; daddy would have spent many days *in the can*. Their fighting was so bad that my brother and I often ran out of the house and down the street, screaming for help! I was mentally traumatized by their violent acts — the first *domino*. I don't think my parents realized how their violent behavior would affect me in the years to come. Childhood trauma causes internal scarring that may raise its head in your adult years.

- A 2018 study by researchers from the University of Wisconsin-Madison reported that early-childhood trauma can ripple directly into a child's molecular structure, causing a biological vulnerability to psychiatric and social problems — the root cause of drug addictions, alcoholism, mental illness, and/or homelessness.

Domino Two: Dysfunctional Parents/Teen Runaway

My mother had escaped, and now it was my turn. Mom's exit was good for her, but it left me in a broken state. I have no memory of my mom during my early childhood. Maybe I have suppressed those memories, but I cannot recall any birthdays, storytelling, or mommy-daughter stuff.

It was midsummer, on a scalding-hot day, when, at 15 years old, I had the audacity to talk back to — and even curse at — my dad. Not only was my mother gone, but my dad's concubine had moved into our home. I had been smoking pot with my friend earlier that day. After smoking our last joint, I headed home — "high as a Georgia pine." Arriving home, I discovered a woman's belongings in boxes, stacked in the living room. Her nightlife dress was strewn across my dad's bed, ready to be hung in the closet. Rage shot through me like a flaming spear. I said, "What the hell is happening here? Am I in the right house?" I double-checked the address. "Yep! I'm in the right place." This bold-ass wench, who used to call my mother on the phone, had *moved into our house.* I wanted to choke somebody!

With my blood boiling, fire in my heart, and bloodshot eyes, I peered out to confront daddy in the front yard. My father stepped out of the car, groceries in hand, and, at that moment, I became bold as hell to speak my mind. I said, "Who are you to let this silly woman move into our home? You've got balls and a lot of nerve. Where is she?" I asked him.

"I don't think it's any of your business. I pay the bills around here," he said.

I was sweating and breathing heavily, high on pot, and I had forgotten to put my shoes on before I went outside. "It's a good thing that mama left your crazy butt, you coward," I scowled at him. "I should have known you were the problem long ago and went with my mother. She was right about you. You ain't about nothin'! Now I understand why mama screamed at this woman over the telephone. How dare you move this whore into our house?" Daddy was turning reddish, and his eyes narrowed in on me as he approached me. *Oh, gosh! I done pissed this man off*, I thought, and, impulsively, I turned toward the street and ran for my life.

I ran down the street barefoot; the gravel road was scorching hot and burned the soles of my feet. Standing in the middle of the street, I cursed away at my dad. Then I heard the engine of the Monte Carlo. He was careening down the street toward me. He got out and began to chase me. I cut to the right and ran off the road into the desert, stepping over the weeds and around cacti, as rocks and goat-heads pierced my soles and my feet sunk in hot sand. My heart was racing as daddy chased me with a 2-by-4 in his hand. I was officially "a teenage runaway."

- As reported on https://www.jsonline.com/story/news/2018/07/19/uw-madison-study-affirms-trauma-creates-genetic-change-endures/797668002/

Domino Three: Substance Abuse

After the chase, I couldn't return to my dad's house. At the time, my maternal grandparents were retiring and relocating to their retirement home in Northern California; they took me in. My Grandma Lou was a devout Christian woman. The move seemed good, but it wasn't because my behavior got worse, but not because of my grandparents. My grandma had a house rule that you had to attend church every Sunday. She had long talks with me about the Lord, and, at the time, I didn't understand.

Then I was introduced to *crack cocaine* and speed-balling with heroin. One thing led to another. I went from smoking crack to selling it on the streets. There were older, big-time dealers who trusted me to sell their product. There is a thin line between using drugs and selling them. If you are a distributor only and not a user, you *might* make it. It's when I began using the problem caused me to spiral down into a deep, dark place that lasted for more than a decade.

- In 2018, there were 4,633 drug-overdose deaths among youths aged 15-24

Domino Four: Depression

Depression affects people differently. Back then, you didn't hear as much about teenage depression as you hear now. I had all the signs. I had low self-esteem and poor performance in school, which led to me being kicked out of regular high school, but I managed to get my diploma while pregnant with my firstborn son.

I moved briefly back to Palm Springs, and I had a suicidal episode under the influence of cocaine and alcohol. I ended up in a mental hospital for a couple of days. This was more than forty years ago.

- Teenage suicide is the second leading cause of death among Americans age 15 to 24.

- Between 2007 and 2017, there was a 59% increase in teenage depression.
  As reported by drugabusestatistics.com
  As reported on pewresearch.org/fact-tank

Domino Five: The Dunamis Domino

As horrific as these events were, *I'm still standing* because of the Dunamis Domino. Dunamis is a Greek term for the power of God in my life. When I was younger, I wondered why I didn't fit in with anyone, but I later read in God's word that I'm *"fearfully and wonderfully"* made and was never meant to fit in. I was a square peg trying to squeeze into a round hole. But when I discovered that God loved me and had so many good things in store for me. I went from dope to hope. I've been clean and sober for more than three decades. God has restored everything that was taken from me.

> *"Life said, 'I'm going to make you happy, but I'm going to make you strong first.'"*
> (Author unknown)

Even at my lowest, most painful moments in life, when all hope seemed lost, I knew that God was just a prayer away. *"Behold, The Lord's hand is not shortened, that it cannot save; neither his ear heavy, that it cannot hear"* (Isaiah 59:1 KJV). I've experienced a total transformation by crying out to God. I'm now a born-again Christian. I've been happily married for 33 years and have raised four sons. I'm a homeowner and a serial entrepreneur — with licenses in multiple industries.

Get your Dunamis (D – O – M – I – N – O)

Take *dominion*. Claim and take back everything that was stolen. Remember: God is *omniscient* — all-wise, sees every situation, and will strategically bring you out. While the *magnitude* of your pain and suffering may have been beyond measure, the rewards from God will outweigh them all. So, be *intentional*, get-up, and take charge of your life. Love and *nurture* yourself on the road to recovery. Don't be *overtaken* but let God's Dunamis power transform your life by first renewing your mind.

Debra A. Bledsoe

Debra wears many hats: wife, mother, and minister. She holds a Bachelor of Arts degree in Journalism and an MBA in Business. Debra is a serial entrepreneur, first, in the Culinary Arts arena, which led her to owning her own catering business. She has been a top-producing real-estate sales professional for more than 22 years. In both her personal life and in her professional career, Debra is passionate about helping others achieve their goals. She is innovative and tech-savvy. Over the years, Debra has accumulated substantial knowledge in various industrial and occupational fields. She is a business and Christian coach, eager to share her wealth of experience and education. Debra is an avid communicator and is currently in the process of writing her first book.

Debra can be reached via email: dblessed29@verizon.net

Lead with Purpose & Live on Purpose®
By Dr. Rakimm Broadnax-Rogers

When you are in your natural element of fulfilling your purpose and accomplishing professional goals and endeavors, you tend to forget about the foundation you are standing on. All too often, we fail to set boundaries to protect the foundation.

For nearly three decades, I had the distinct honor of serving our country as a Combat Veteran. With this great honor, I was blessed to lead at strategic levels of influence, with an unmatched opportunity to shape a narrative well beyond my humble beginnings. The narrative that I was not prepared to shape was how to navigate the next chapter of my life successfully. Specifically, how to pivot from one spectrum of my life to another, with a seamless transition.

Despite leading and inspiring thousands to lead with a purpose and live on purpose, I was paralyzed with fear. Without hesitation, I knew this self-discovery journey and transition from my career as a professional Soldier would not yield a seamless transition. Rather, this would expose weaknesses, threats, missed opportunities, and unmitigated chaos suppressed for well over two decades. Inevitably, I would place myself in a position that I took great pride in professionally, taking accountability, and owning your truth.

It is a horrific undertaking to reconcile the fact you built a system of accountability to others and left the most important aspect out, being accountable to yourself, first and foremost. I want to pay it forward and share with you my sustainable life strategy. I am still standing after recognizing my lack of being present in the moment, as a result of carrying two decades of toxic baggage. My strategy empowered me to pivot from fear and to master the art of leading in my own life with a sense of purpose while living on purpose.

"Finding balance is a method; finding purpose is a must."
Rakimm Broadnax-Rogers

Draw a distinct line in the sand

When you draw the line, and others cross it, don't relegate yourself to an inferior position and draw another line. Release yourself from the guilt of not making concessions; when someone makes a deliberate decision to dishonor your boundaries, it's not worth the emotional investment.

Don't wait for autonomy

It's your life, you can't wait for someone to give you permission to lead your most important mission. If you wait for someone to validate your decisions, you are essentially allowing someone to acknowledge and analyze your capacity and capability.

When I rendered the decision to retire from a successful career, it defied all logic. I was at the top of my career and enjoying the fruits of my labor. I can recall every aspect of that pivotal decision. My alarm went off at 4:15 a.m.; this time, I did not get up and start my routine. Rather, I pondered what I could gain from taking a detour in life after consistently executing the same task for nearly three decades. I didn't rationalize my thoughts or go through my normal list of doubts. I went into my office and submitted two documents, a retirement request effective six months from the date of submission, and a request to take a few days off. I knew with the immediate time away; I could detach from the world and shield myself from the frivolous questions about my decision. I knew all external communication would mobilize fear, potentially causing me to doubt my decision and essentially release my autonomy to someone else.

Adjust your sights/Get a good sight picture

If you have ever shot a rifle, there are fundamental skills to consider such as adjusting your sight. When you adjust the sights, it is for your individual benefit and tailored to what you see. Any sudden movements or jolts during transport or storage can knock a rifle out of alignment. The same holds true as you are preparing to transition to your next level of greatness. There will be an external distractor waiting to knock you out of alignment from your destiny. You must adjust your sights based on the milestones you wish to accomplish on your journey. It takes relentless commitment and a laser-focused approach; any sudden movement of self-doubt, unsolicited opinions from non-stakeholders can knock you out of alignment.

"Lead with a purpose & Live on purpose."
Rakimm Broadnax-Rogers

Busy is not related to productive

Being busy and being productive are not interchangeable; in fact, both are like distant relatives meeting for the first time at a family gathering. Most will equate being busy to being productive; that is far from the reality of how you are performing. If you have set an intentional mark to transition to another realm of greatness in your life, you must be willing to take inventory and discover the unvarnished truth.

Why have you been busy?

Who benefited from your constant state of busyness?

What was the return on investment? Did this constant state of busyness yield productivity to take you into the next spectrum of your life, or were you essentially building capacity for others. If you were busy building capacity for others, did you take a strategic pause to recognize at some point they may not have the ability to reciprocate and how you would react?

Accept progress over perfection

Real healing transpires when we set boundaries outside of our comfort zone. If you identify as a perfectionist, be prepared to go through an identity crisis. When you aspire to discover unchartered territory, and leave your comfort zone, embrace the intimate moments that define your strengths and weaknesses. Life begins at the end of our comfort zone, make the shift, and accept progress over perfection. Celebrate the small wins; a new mindset equates to new results.

Access Denied

If you have attempted to add a program to a computer in your place of employment, chances are you have seen the following message "Access Denied! Windows can't optimize the drive because you're not signed in as Administrator." You must challenge yourself to place your life and this journey of self-discovery in the same context. If you fell into a position of allowing others to dictate how you live or you lived to satisfy the needs of others, essentially, they were the administrator. You will need to do a hard reboot, take your rightful position, and become selective on who you provide administrator rights to. Before you delegate and grant this level of access, it's important, measure how someone will use this privilege. You must be willing to invest the requisite time to measure the intentions of others, are their intentions aligned with building your foundation, or exposing cracks in your foundation. You cannot optimize what you don't measure.

> *"Make the decision today to own your tomorrow."*
> Rakimm Broadnax-Rogers

Don't put a question mark where there is a period

I have spent countless hours analyzing moments in life where I did not have superior qualifications, yet I was placed in positions and given opportunities to build a sustainable future for those I was blessed to lead and my family. What I have learned is you don't have to be the most qualified; you just need to change your mindset and be willing to embrace the opportunity. Embrace the opportunities that come your way, claim your success in advance.

Don't build capacity with substandard capability

When you accept this new season in your life, accept the fact you may need to rebuild either partially or fully. This rebuild may align with gaining a new skill or soliciting the help of a professional in your new area of focus. Time is your most valuable commodity. You must be willing to invest in a professional that can reduce your learning curve or a seasoned coach to reaffirm your desires to exemplify excellence in action. While you are building capacity for this next level of greatness, take a stand and know that you can't build capacity with substandard capability. There are some toxic elements, and even people not fitting to accompany you on your journey.

Distinguish between happiness and freedom and allow freedom to prevail

If everything were designed to be easy, we would be prepared for our destiny. I often counted happiness and freedom as being synonymous; that is far from the truth. Once I completed the necessary work, I had to face the harsh reality that I spent an absorbent amount of time making others happy at the cost of my freedom. Happiness is contentment or a form of satisfaction, which is temporary in nature. Freedom is the absence of necessity. I no-longer found the necessity of meeting the request of others at the expense of my freedom. When you let go and claim your freedom, you will come to appreciate this new level of clarity and fearlessness. You are the next success story; if not now, when?

Turn your face to the sun, and the shadows fall behind you
- Maori Proverb

Dr. Rakimm Broadnax-Rogers

Dr. Rakimm Broadnax-Rogers is a Combat Veteran with nearly three decades of dedicated service to the nation. As a servant leader, Dr. Broadnax-Rogers continues to serve as an Associate Professor, Leadership/Success Coach and as a Diversity and Inclusion Executive. Dr. Broadnax-Rogers is a purpose driven thought leader. Through coaching, Dr. Broadnax-Rogers empowers her clients to reach their fullest potential and discover their purpose. The essence of her work is to facilitate self-growth by helping her clients identify their core challenges and setbacks, so they can overcome them with confidence. Dr. Broadnax-Rogers takes a relentless approach to her life strategy of "Lead with purpose & Live on Purpose"®.

You can connect with Dr. Broadnax-Rogers
Instagram: @rakimmbr1
https://www.spectrum2spectrum.com/

It's Not Always About Me
By Sharon J. Bullock

My childhood best friend, Donna, is still in my life until this day. We grew up together in Gainesville, GA, and from sixth grade forward, we were inseparable. Although we live miles apart, we stay in touch and will always be there for each other. We went to different colleges and made new friends.

Donna attended schools in Georgia, and in 1973, I transferred from Morris Brown College in Atlanta to Morgan State (which became MSU) in Maryland. **This is where I met Cherie'.** She was one of the first people I met at Morgan, and we hit it off instantly! She became my college best friend and beyond. She and other friends at MSU nicknamed me 'Georgia.' She never called me anything else. She was the matron of honor for both of my marriages. We knew each other's deep, dark secrets. She was my confidante, my counselor, my shoulder to cry on, and I loved her so very much.

I only remember two major disagreements we had over our 40 years plus relationship. One of them put a damper on our friendship. I thought it was so trivial at the time. Someone asked me to be in an MLM selling supplements and thought Cherie' would be a great candidate since she was a Personal Trainer. The kicker was, this person asked me, "Doesn't she support you in your business?" Keep in mind, I did not know Cherie' did not like this particular person, and I forgot she also hated supplements! It made me question Cherie's loyalty and support. Since I had been trying to start a business and she knew all these VIPs, I thought maybe I should ask why she hadn't supported me in my businesses, as this person suggested. OMG, after this episode, although we were still close, things were never the same, which caused a little distance between us. We went from talking every day to weekly monthly and then, whenever.

The other major disagreement was the year before she died. We were still close but had grown somewhat apart, partially due to our busy schedules and our other sets of friends. I was overly passionate about the boutique I had opened in 2007. I spent most of my time trying to save it after the 2008 recession and my dream home we had built the same year but ended up losing them both. Cherie' was diagnosed with a rare lung cancer. In the beginning, she had gotten the best care and treatment and was in remission for some time. Since we spoke less, and each time we did, she seemed to be doing well; I soon forgot she was sick.

I became so consumed with my work and staying afloat that I was calling her less, and she was the one calling me at times. One day I called, and she did not call me back. This was October 2014, it was It was Homecoming month, and it was the 40th Anniversary of her line. We had both pledged Delta Sigma Theta Sorority at MSU, and my line had celebrated our 40th the year before. I thought it was a great time to call and catch up. I kept trying and finally spoke with her. When I asked why she did not call me back, she lashed out at me for not calling and reminded me she had CANCER! Since I had been so out of touch and no one else ever called me either, I assumed she was well and even actually thought she was cured! Unbeknownst to me, she had relapsed, and the cancer was back full force. I felt so devastated! I had abandoned her. She called me a "fair-weathered friend".

By then, I had already lost my home and was on the verge of losing my business too. I could not share what I had been through and how it led to my deep depression. I could not tell her I had not called anyone because of my despair and how I was too depressed to even attend my first husband's mother's funeral, whom I was close to as well. Nothing could compare with her cancer. I was at a loss for words. I begged her to forgive me. I promised to do better. However, my time was running out to save my business. I became laser-focused on this, and time passed again between us. I think we spoke one or two other times.

Later in December 2014, I lost my business and went into another deep depression. I lashed out at everyone around me, my husband and my cousin who stayed with us at the time. I did not call anyone. I did not know what to do with my life now. I was losing everything. For days I would sit in my bedroom looking at the four walls. Before I knew it, the day had passed, and I had accomplished nothing! One day in the Spring of 2015, I passed through Bethesda MD and thought I should stop and see Cherie'. Then I thought, she must really hate me by now, and I did not want to be rejected, so I talked myself out of it. I tried calling her again, but she did not call back. By then, she must have been deteriorating and getting worse, but I had no idea. I never physically saw or spoke to her again.

A month or two later, a mutual friend called and asked me, "Is it true about Cherie'?" My heart skipped a beat. I had just started this new job unrelated to my passion and was in training at the time. I asked, "Was what true?" She said she heard Cherie' had passed! I dropped the phone in so much pain. I was never the same again. The guilt engulfed me. I was too ashamed to call her husband, her mother, or her daughter. I wondered, "What did they think of me? What kind of friend was I to abandon her like this?" I did call her sister Wendy and expressed my condolences, and I spoke to our mutual friend Judy. She assured me she would keep me posted about the arrangements. This was in May 2015.

I went through another depression riddled with profound guilt and gut-wrenching shame. I could not explain why I was not there for her in the end. I was told Cherie' would be cremated, and they would have a memorial service around her birthday in July 2015. In June, I went to a conference in Dallas, Texas. While there, I called Judy to ask when the memorial was going to be. She told me Cherie's family had a private service for her the day before! I completely lost it! I was in a restaurant and just could not hold back the tears. She told me it was by invitation only. I thought, maybe it came while I was out of town. There is no way I was not invited! I immediately called my husband. I told him what happened as I was weeping and filled with distress. He told me he thought something came, and he had accidentally thrown it away. Later I would find out he lied to make me feel better. I was never invited. Maybe she wanted it this way and told them not to put me on the list. After all, I was not there for her! I had no idea how to make this up to her. She was gone now, and I would have to live with this truth for the rest of my life.

A day does not go by that I don't think about her and how we were during the good times. On her birthday, July 10, 2015, I had my own memorial service for her at my friend Elena's studio. I read a letter I wrote to her asking for her forgiveness and tied it to a bouquet of balloons and released them to heaven with her.

I never got the courage to call her husband and tell him how sorry I was, but I later ran into him at another memorial service at my church. We immediately hugged, and I felt his forgiveness without either of us speaking a word. The good news is, I saw a picture of their beautiful daughter, Hilary, on Facebook, and I made a comment. She immediately responded, and we ended up meeting for lunch and spending the day together. I shared what happened and poured out my soul to her. We wept together, and I found out they did not hate me at all. They thought I hated them! We still text each other now and then, and I will never let her out of my life as I watch her grow into the beautiful woman she has become and is still becoming. Cherie's legacy lives on, and it's not always about me...

Sharon J. Bullock

Sharon J. Bullock is a Wardrobe Coach & Stylist, Makeup Artist, and Color Analyst with over 40 years in the Beauty & Fashion Industry. She is the Visionary Author of **Embracing My Sexy Sixties!** and former owner of Metamorphosis Wardrobe & Accessories Boutique. Sharon is a graduate of Morgan State University and a member of Delta Sigma Theta Sorority, Inc. She is also the Co-Founder & Vice President of Sisters 4 Sisters Network, Inc. She is a member of Entrepreneurs & Professionals Network (EPNET), Bold, Brave & Beautiful, a member of eWomen Network, Women Business Owners, Circle of Champions, and Women Business Network of America. She is the recipient of numerous awards including the Top 100 MBEs (Minority Business Enterprises) Award, Washington Business Journal Minority Business Leaders Award, Black Capitol Awards II, Be There Magazine's Trailblazer award, and many more.

https://www.facebook.com/sharon.j.bullock
https://www.instagram.com/sharonjbullock/
www.embracingmysexysixties.com
sharon@embracingmysexysixties.com

The Silent Killer: Workplace BULLYING
By Rochelle A. Campbell, MA

It was like walking into a turbulent ocean (the office) with ferocious sharks (managers/enemies) surrounding you on every side. I was treading water in a forceful and steady movement, yet I could not gain my footing. The uncertainty of the malice and unpredictable behaviors, excessive assignments, and antagonistic meetings caused fear that you will be devoured alive (psychologically and emotionally) by every move you made. This force would trigger one's self-doubt and deplete their self- esteem severely. This experience proved to be one of the worst times of my life.

What was this experience? While this was happening, it was silently killing me. I was a victim of bullying in the workplace: mental attacks, mistreatment, defamation of character, ill will, and micro-aggressive behaviors. It caused me to have self-doubt, and the treatment severely wounded my self-esteem.

Somebody developed a well-constructed process that would damage every part of a person's life. All the sharks (managers) knew their role. It all started with a few random projects; then, it would later grow to receive an enormous amount of new work projects sent through email. I had constant chimes on my calendar for work reminders for work assignments that had staggering due dates. I was given a vast amount of work without guidance, direction, or training. Somebody would schedule impromptu meetings, and tasks were picked apart repeatedly, not a mistake made on my part, but used to diminish me personally. On any given day, I would be spoken to or yelled at forcefully, "ARE YOU INCOMPETENT"!!!!! IS THERE SOMETHING WRONG WITH YOU?

The office became an official place of anxiety and strife for me. The office began to be driven continuously by abuse and malevolence. I was unable to focus, unable to connect, unable to find solace as to why this was happening to me. The workplace consumed my life with apprehension. By the end of every week, I would start thinking of reasons to call out for the following week.

So, I reached out and asked family, friends, and my physician for HELP! But nothing seemed to click. Nothing made sense. Even the common-sense responses provided did not benefit me. Here are a few options provided "if I were you .... I would (cuss them out, beat them up, go to your superior ".) None of these options seemed rational, as I still wanted to maintain my professionalism, good work ethic, and demeanor. All of that sounded great, but it wasn't the best course of action at the time for me!

After the year of bondage in a toxic workplace, there was still no resolve. I completed all my assignments and all of the extra work in most cases before the due date. It still wasn't good enough. Everything that was happening was set up for me to fail. I almost lost my mind. I would lose a large part of my life! They took everything from me that I worked so hard to get. Just like that- it was all taken from me - my title, office, and salary. I felt like I was in a million little pieces. The millionth piece caused my breaking point. I decided to take a leave of absence. Time away was going to be my refuge, my safety, my oasis. Once I got to the shore's safety, I decided not to be concerned about anything but regaining my sanity. My ONLY focus was to become rebalanced.

This course of action would surprise the sharks (managers/enemies) as I swam to shore.

During the time away from the office, I had more time to reflect on all that was going on. I spoke to God regularly and was confused as to why this was happening to me. Why would I have to put up such a fight for the wrong others were doing to me? Why would somebody want me to fail intentionally? I had to fight for an understanding, purpose, and my voice!

So, one day I asked GOD ... GOOOOOODah, why me? A clear, concise, and piercing answer returned in my spirit WHY NOT YOU? That day restarted my life and a new purposeful journey. I began to rebuild, refocus, rebirth my FAITH, purpose, and understanding of this storm, and rebuild a stronger relationship with God. I began to read and intensely study the word (sword). I learned to listen to the creator.

I was intentional and prepared to clear my heart, free my mind, and get ready for the journey God prepared for me. I was taking the best course of action as I focused on God's word. I used journaling to capture my feelings and thoughts throughout my journey, speaking his name over my life and the lives of my enemies, keeping my heart and mind clear of rubbish. He allowed me to understand that he would fight my battles, and as long as I stayed connected to him through his word, which would later become the power (sword). God's words killed everything harmful around me. His power provided a supernatural grace over my life. At one point, my finances became VERY unstable. I began to lose hope after my leave was exhausted, and one of my last checks posted was $19.00. My family would often ask if I needed money for my mortgage, car, or food. But I would soon realize that no one ever asked if I need toiletries, those items we all need and use every single day. So, I became laser-focused on following my heart. I asked GOD, was this my purpose in this storm? I began to research to see if organizations solely focused on helping with toiletry items (basic care needs). In my search, none popped up. I began to get connected to everything I needed. I would later start a non-profit, Toiletry and Company, Inc. We provide personal care items to assist those in need year-round throughout the world. Oh, and the $19.00 check by GOD'S grace kept me. I never lacked food and never received a disconnection notice for my household utilities.

You see, now I was on the shore watching the (managers/enemies) circle in the water, under the protection of God's favor and grace. I saw how God's words fought, kept me, and helped me to rebalance, to rebuild and refocus spiritually, psychologically, and emotionally to withstand the fight of my life. In that fight, I made an oath that I would always trust in GOD and follow his plans to free us by using the words to guide, prepare, and sustain us throughout life's journey. I made confessions to read and live by his name. My trip came full circle with the use of scriptures and affirmational actions that I live by and continue to use while focusing on this journey.

I learned to use affirmational actions continually over my life.

1. Be focused on GOD

2. Always Be HUMBLE

3. Always be GRATEFUL from soap to your salary

4. Have FAITH/FEAR, LOVE over HATE

5. I WORK for GOD and not for humans

6. I PRAY before I REACT

7. TAKE these words out of your vocabulary ANGER, REVENGE, and STRIFE

By reading His Word (sword) daily and building a stronger relationship with GOD, I have discovered a feeling of peace in my heart and a cleared mind that passes all understanding.

Hello, my name is Rochelle and, I was a victim of workplace bullying.

I AM finally at PEACE and not in pieces.

Rochelle A. Campbell, MA

Rochelle A. Campbell is the Executive Director of Toiletry and Company, Inc. This community-based organization serves as an epicenter for personal care items for under-served populations residing in the community and residential programs (i.e., veterans, domestic violence, homeless, and youth facilities) and is committed to providing an opportunity for individuals to meet their essential daily needs for living.

She holds a Bachelor of Science in Rehabilitation Services from the University of Maryland- Eastern Shore and a Master of Art in Counseling Psychology from Bowie State University.

Rochelle has a unique approach in how she has chosen to make a difference in this world, coupled with her spirit of giving and skill for community organizing; she lives by the motto, "service above self."

Contact:
FB: Toiletry and Company, Inc.
IG: Toiletry@1
www.toiletryandco.org
toiletryandcompany@gmail.com

Demons In The Bedroom
By Tesha D. Colston

I knew it was coming, but I had a plan, a way of escape, I was sure would work. I thought I would go into my daughter's bedroom, lay across her bed, and go to sleep. That plan didn't work, and he was literally trying to have sex with me in my daughters' bed, but my thighs were strong. So, he pulled me by my feet through the hall and into our bedroom.

We have four children, three of whom were home, and no one came to my rescue. They were either sleeping or had become numb to the fussing. So, no one even came out of their room to see what was going on. The daughter, whose room I was in, pretended to be asleep, but there was no way she could be. It was probably for the best for them that they all remained silent. At this point, it was like there was a demon that had taken him over.

My first husband was verbally, physically, and sexually abusive during our twenty-five years of marriage. I thought his behavior would change, but it never did. I had no one to talk to. How could I discuss these things? I was ashamed and afraid and had no one coming to my rescue. I tried to talk to leaders in the church, but in the end, they didn't really know how to handle it. So, I kept on working, and I kept on ministering to others. I kept on leading, and I kept on living through it all.

How It started

I do not remember the first time this happened. I do not remember the first time my husband raped me. I remember the jealousy that had gotten worse as time went on. I remember fights because there were a lot of them. He was extremely jealous, and he would accuse me of sleeping with everyone, and that jealousy never ended. When he got into one of his fits of jealousy, he would always want sex, and there is where the fights would start. I didn't know it was rape at the time, but I knew it wasn't right. I knew marriage wasn't supposed to be this way.

Why didn't I leave?

Just like people wondered why those in domestic violence situations don't leave, I also wondered why I wouldn't just leave for good. Over the course of our marriage, I did leave a few times; I just didn't stay gone. I admit the times I left were only after the police had been called, and an order of protection was issued. He was very good at apologizing and begging me to come back. Also, as I look back, I never considered myself as a domestic violence victim. Besides, it was all my fault, right? I mean, if I would just have sex when he wanted, most of this wouldn't have happened, right? Then there is how to leave? What would I do? It wasn't that bad, I thought. I made this bed, and I need to lay in it. I kept getting pregnant, and because I didn't want any more children, I would have abortions. I lost count on how many I had; I believe I had about seven in the first seven years of marriage.

He was so jealous he just accused me of sleeping with every man we knew. He wanted sex all the time, and I wanted it none of the time. I was miserable. The physical abuse was never constant. The sexual abuse was never consistent. I had learned to give in, and I stopped fighting as much.

One of my coping mechanisms throughout my marriage was drugs and alcohol, which he introduced me to. We smoked a lot of marijuana, drank beer and alcohol, did cocaine, and we would watch porn. See, if

I could just be in the mood, I wouldn't get into trouble, and so down that path of addiction I continued.

Eventually, I started going to church, and I found some peace in that. Maybe if I'm going to church, it would stop. Maybe this foolishness would stop, but it didn't, but at least I had hope;, I now had God. I hoped God would protect me. Maybe the more I attended church, the more I would earn his protection, but that was the wrong way to think, and my situation did not change.

I remember being so depressed; I would fight off the thoughts of suicide. I had children to be here for. However, there is this one time that I remember getting up in the middle of the night, getting a knife, and coming back to the bed. I had enough of this life, and I was going to end it. I was going to leave, just not the way I should have left. So, I laid down with the intent to slit my wrist and bleed out over the very bed I had had so much pain. I heard a voice that stopped me and quoted scripture saying, "weeping may endure for a night, but joy comes in the morning. If you hang on in the morning, you won't feel this way. Your problems will still be there, but you won't feel this way." So, I put the knife down and went to sleep. This is the victory... I got up!

How it ended...

I was in denial about the severity of my situation. I compared my situation to others. I mean, I wasn't one of the women who had black and blue eyes and ended up in the hospital with fractures and swollen faces. No, this abuse, this pain no one could see. Society and church have very different views on this type of abuse. It was not ok to be not ok with sex in marriage. Your body is not your own. You should tell your husband yes, all the time. It's your fault.

One day, my youngest son had brought home a pamphlet that talked about domestic violence. It listed out all the ways people are abused. Verbal and sexual abuse were on the list. It was then that I realized that

I victim of domestic violence, I was not alone, and it was not OK with everyone.

I had a conversation with my husband about it. I told him that what he was doing was actually rape and that he could go to jail for rape. He didn't believe me. I showed him the pamphlet. I think I had hoped that it would stop, and we would have a normal relationship, but it didn't. This time, during the act, I could tell him he was raping me, but that never worked.

Fast forward to the day the washer broke, and I needed to go to my cousin's apartment to wash clothes. I took one of my daughters with me. We had a lot of clothes, and I was there for a long time. I don't know why I didn't go to the Laundromat, but we were there so long we all fell asleep and didn't get home until the next morning.

I knew he would be upset, but I didn't think he would be that mad after all, I was washing our clothes, and I had my daughter with me. He argued, but the kids were home, and I was like, man, you are tripping. The kids got ready for school, and off they went. There's where the real arguing happened. I remember he had me pinned to the wall with his hands around my throat, telling me he could kill me. I don't remember all the details. I just know the police were called. This time they didn't arrest him, but he chose to leave. I had made the final decision; I was just done.

I packed some things and off I went to my cousin's house. I stayed there and guess what he did? He filed for divorce, and I never went back!

What is Domestic Violence?

Domestic violence is not just punching and hitting. It can also come in forms others never see. "The traditional definition of rape in the United States is the forced sexual intercourse by a male with a "female, not his wife," making it clear that the statutes did not apply to married couples." (Wikipedia.org) Today, marital rape is illegal in all 50 states. Marital rape was criminalized in 1983.

What to Do If You Have Been Sexually Violated in Your Marriage?

Reach out for help! Even if you feel alone, try to reach out to someone. For any victims and survivors of DV who need support, the Domestic Violence Hotline is available 24 hours a day, 7 days a week, at 1-800-799-7233 or 1-800-787-3224 for TTY. If you're unable to speak safely, you can log onto hotline.org or text LOVEIS to 22522.

Look for my book coming in 2021 for more about "Demons in The Bedroom."

Tesha D. Colston

Tesha D. Colston is a Certified Life & Financial Coach, Speaker, and Author. Tesha has more than 15 years' experience in Christian ministry. She also has 20 years of Corporate Training and Facilitation, Call Center Management, and Supervision experience.

Tesha wears one hat with many experiences and gifts. Her passion is to show women how to partner with God in her finances to achieve financial freedom so that she can create a life she loves to live.

Tesha's life journey has equipped her with unique messages filled with compassion and simplicity. She encourages women in a way that empowers growth.

Tesha D. Colston is married to Kenneth J. Colston and together they have 6 children and 8 grandchildren.

Tesha can be found on the internet at www.teshadcolston.com and on social media by searching for teshadcolston.

Constantly Pouring From An Empty Cup Lead Me To Self-Care
By Chernika L. Corbett

It was June 26, 2019. This was the start of my life-changing physically, mentally, and emotionally. The day started like any other; I made my long commute to work and sat at my desk, preparing for my day. I remember not feeling well. I was a little dizzy, and my head was hurting. I chalked it up to just another headache that will go away once I pop those Excedrin. My boss walked in and said, you don't look well, Chernika. You're really pale. I told her I had a slight headache, and I would be fine. However, my boss insisted that I have my blood pressure checked by one of the nurses to be on the safe side, and I agreed. Once they checked my blood pressure, it read 230/190, which was extremely dangerous, and was told I needed to be transported to the hospital immediately. I called Monike, my sister, and my fiancé Harvey to advise them that I was being transported to the hospital. That was the last thing that I remembered.

Apparently, I had been in the hospital for 12 hours. When I woke up to Harvey sitting by my bedside, it made me smile, but it also made me sad. It made me sad because I had no control. I felt helpless, and like I couldn't accomplish anything by being laid up in a hospital bed. Harvey said it was unacceptable because I was way more important, not just to him but to my daughters and family and giving up is not an option. Whatever support I needed, he said he had me no matter what. I was happy to be alive, but I had so many questions. The one that stuck out the most was, WHY ME? When I was advised I would be in the hospital until they could get my blood pressure under control, I was like, this is not the move right now. I was ready to go, but the doctor said, don't ask when you're leaving because this is not something that can be rushed. I guess God said, "you weren't seeing all the signs I was giving you, so I had to take you out for a minute. This is your wake-up call." It took me out, but as we all know, sometimes being stubborn, hardheaded, and acting like you are invincible just makes your road to recovery harder than it has to be.

A week later, I was out of the hospital and hit the ground running. In my head, I was fine and could go back to work and resume my normal life. I started doing my normal running around running the business, doing everything for everyone like I wasn't just in the hospital. I noticed I was starting to get the constant headaches again, and that's when reality set in; I wasn't ready. I stayed up late at night crying because I felt like I failed people around me because being sick was not an option; slowing down was not an option. I was the person that made things move, and I made things happen on so many different levels. If I couldn't do that, it meant I failed on all those levels. I started to ask what is wrong with me and wondered why I couldn't bounce back like normal. It was so damn frustrating. This made me snap at people and isolate myself unless it had to do with running the business. People would see me smiling, laughing, and joking, but I had become good at hiding my feelings and emotions. I got so good at it; I was hiding it from myself. I was self-destructing and ignoring all the signs, yet again.

Since I couldn't go back to work without clearance from the doctor, my fiancé and I went away to California. It was the first time I felt at peace in so long. It was like I had no care in the world. I sat on the beach and wrote everything that I was feeling in my journal, and it was like a weight lifted. I knew then I needed to work on me and healing myself. It didn't matter how many times people talked to me about taking care of me; I needed to recognize it for myself. That, of course, was easier said than done. The way I'm set up, I didn't know how to relax and work on me. I just knew how to tell others how to do it and how important it was not just for adults but also for kids. I felt like a hypocrite because I was promoting self-care/self-love, but I wasn't doing the same for me. After feeling sorry for myself for way too long, I started my journey of self-care/self-love. I begin to take my journal writing seriously and take the time to meditate, pray, and celebrate my life and myself for the Queen that I am. While doing this, I noticed a change in myself that I loved. It felt good to be at peace.

I was loving this journey-things to be going well for me mentally, physically, and emotionally. One day on my commute to work, I got a text that my Uncle Ben had passed. I was feeling all kinds of emotions, with sadness being right at the top. On my way home the same day, my Uncle Tima had to be rushed to the hospital after a fall. When it happened, I didn't know that my uncle would never come home again. I felt like my anxiety was getting the best of me. Losing another uncle couldn't be happening right now. While preparing for my uncle's funeral, I received another call that my aunt Jeanette passed away. My heart broke, my tears took over, and I felt like, why is this happening? Why is God taking away all the good people? How can you get over one death when another hits you? At this point, I couldn't even function correctly. I was scared to look at my text or answer a phone call from my family in fear of it being more bad news. Fear had taken over, and that was hard to beat.

After burying my family members, it bought my cousins and I closer. We created a group chat to remain in touch even when we are far away from each other. This was good for me because I had begun to struggle with taking care of myself yet again. Death can affect you positively or negatively. Sometimes it is easier to take the negative route when you are already struggling emotionally. My fiancé stayed on top of me about handling stress and helping with ways to cope with my losses. He was the strong person in my life who made sure I was always good. I also had a Queen, Charmyra, who always gave me reassuring advice and was supportive through this challenging time. Tears and all, she never judged but was resilient, which was so needed.

Here I was working to get back on track after the self-sabotaging, the deaths, and feeling like giving up on it all. I have learned that I was constantly giving and giving and giving, and I never realized that I wasn't giving to myself. As long as everyone else was good, then that was great, but I left me out of the equation each and every time. Now I take time for myself. I'm consistent with my meditation and making sure I take care of me first, and everything else follows and falls into place. I stay surrounded by a positive tribe with no exceptions. I'm not completely healed, but I'm on the right track for healing positively. Keya, my spiritual guide, has been a huge help in learning how to heal and balancing my Chakras. I appreciate her so much for that.

My story is for those who don't value themselves and have trouble practicing self-care. Some ways that I believe that can help you is knowing that self-care is also self-love. You want to take care of yourself from the inside out. You want to always have a cup that runs over and never pour from a cup that is half full or empty. This is when you see yourself in a different light, and doors will open. After all, you are able to handle anything because your cup is running over.

To all my Queens, when you are feeling down, stressed out, and overwhelmed; say it, write it down, and memorize:

I decided I'm going to stop being sad and be a goddess of love and light. A queen of resilience & power and a warrior of bold fearlessness.

Straighten your Crown and Conquer!

Chernika L. Corbett

I'm Chernika L. Corbett and I'm the owner of DeJa Vu Skin. I'm a mom, fiancé, sister, and aunt. I love to travel, read, cook, and spend time with my family. I worked as a Case Manager for the Homeless population for ten years and became a certified domestic violence counselor working with battered women as well as men. I still help out on the emergency hotline for domestic violence when needed. These days you can find me supporting my passion along with my family, creating quality products for myself as well as for others. I also send out positive affirmations to women daily to keep them uplifted and feeling great about themselves. I believe that self-care is a priority and not a luxury. It should be practiced daily in order to be at peace mentally, physically, and emotionally.

Website: www.dejavuskin.com,
Email: nikki@dejavuskin.com,
Social Media: https://www.instagram.com/dejavuskin18/,
https://www.facebook.com/dejavuskin18/

Speaking Almost Took My Last Breath
By Constance Craig-Mason

Three hundred thirty-one thousand four hundred ninety-seven dollars and sixty cents ($331,497.60) is how much was billed to Carefirst Blue Cross and Blue Shield on my behalf over just 16 months! Can we all agree that this is A LOT of money, especially to be spent on healthcare? And what kind of condition(s) would you expect for someone to have when that much money is paid out? The CDC has a list of the most expensive chronic diseases to treat, including heart disease and stroke, cancer, diabetes, obesity, arthritis, Alzheimer's disease, epilepsy, and even dental disease!

Did I have any of these conditions? Nope! But I still nearly lost my life at the age of 40 years old, while doing what I absolutely love to do! Bungee-jumping? No! Kayaking over a waterfall? Uh, nope! Swimming with the sharks? Ma'am/ sir, are you crazy? I was SPEAKING! Yes, that's right, traveling around in and out of states speaking, teaching, empowering, and inspiring others. I know.. A real risk-taker, right? Allow me to share with you how I racked up 255 medical claims, including 28 EKGs, 26 x-rays, 17 CT scans, five ultrasounds, and two MRIs in a year and a half!

Everything was going great. I remember it like it was yesterday. It was about a week after my 40th birthday in May 2019. I was super-excited to be turning 40! I was happily married for 14 years. I was looking good, feeling great, my financial services business was thriving, and my four kids were all grown! I had a sweet little granddaughter, who was almost four years old, and my daughter had a bun in the oven; a grandson! Happy was an understatement. I was ecstatic!

And then, out of nowhere, depression crept up on me like a lion sneaking up on a gazelle. I was fine, and before I knew it, it had grabbed ahold of me! I would lay in bed for hours on end and stay in my bedroom all day for days. I had lost about 10 pounds. I couldn't sleep at night. I couldn't be intimate with my husband. I was either indifferent or overly emotional. I was unbalanced, that's for sure. I canceled speaking engagements and wasn't seeing clients. I dreaded reading my emails, texts and ignored social media notifications (those that KNOW me know that this is a RED flag right here!). I told my husband, "I need to get some help, like right now. I don't care if I have to go into an inpatient program; I will do it. I can't keep going on like this!"

I made an appointment with my new family doctor and shared with her what was going on. She made a referral for me to see a mental health therapist at her office and told me that someone would reach out to me. She put me on Prozac to help me with my depression. Honey, I was right back in that office a week later because that Prozac had taken my libido away, and hubby was not happy about that! Plus, my other symptoms remained. I was literally in that lady's office in tears. She knew she had to do something fast! She got me an appointment with mental health, but it was a week away. Sheesh, I was in crisis. I left and went into the parking lot to make some calls to find my own solution.

I found a partial hospitalization program, where I went to group counseling sessions three days a week for six hours a day. Once a week, I met with the psychiatrist, who went over my progress and prescribed medicine to get me stabilized. Even though I needed help and was glad to have found a place to get it, I quietly sat in there with my hair unkempt, a cap on, no makeup, wrinkled clothes, fuzzy socks, Crocs with my arms folded. But what I loved about this program was that even though all the patients were very different, we still found commonality as adults just trying to make the best of our lives. We could see growth in each other day by day.

The psychiatrist ordered a DNA test that would tell us exactly how my DNA impacts various mental health medications' effectiveness. The lab test is called GeneSight Psychotropic. Wow! Now, I could be placed on the right medicines for my DNA! Perfect, right? Yes, but then, all hell broke loose in my body. After about three weeks of going to my mental health program, I started waking up with chest pain when I breathed in, shortness of breath, and had gained 20 pounds as a side effect from one of the mental health medicines! I had to figure out where this chest pain was coming from. And this started a whirlwind of back and forth emergency room visits!

I started going to the ER in mid-June 2019. They thought it was acid reflux and sent me home after giving me a reflux cocktail. I came back the next week with the same symptoms. They said I might have strained my chest wall from lifting something and sent me home to take an anti-inflammatory. Fine! The mental health meds were getting me up, and out of bed, so I went back to doing what I love. Speaking! From June 22, 2019 – June 30, 2019, I completed five speaking engagements! I was on a roll...

But then my symptoms had gotten worse, and I returned on July 4, 2019. At that point, I was hospitalized for the first time with chest pain, white blood count over 21,000, and infiltrates in my lungs. I had bacterial pneumonia, pericarditis, and sepsis! Why didn't they believe me all the weeks before when I was complaining about these symptoms?

About a week after being discharged, I held my quarterly workshop, "Who's On Your Financial Dream Team: Business Owner's Edition!" I was so happy to be feeling better! And even though I was 156 pounds (20 pounds of weight gain), I was grateful to have survived pneumonia and able to get back to teaching and empowering others! I even did a virtual telesummit in early August 2019. But then I ended up back in the ER for the same symptoms. I had pneumonia again. They gave me an antibiotic and sent me on my way.

In September 2019, I felt better and prepared for a trip to Houston, Texas, for a huge conference where I would be a keynote speaker! But just three days before, I went to the ER for pain and warmth in my right arm. And bam! I had two blood clots in my arm from taking birth control for years, living a mostly sedentary lifestyle. A blood test revealed a genetic blood clotting disorder called Factor V Leiden also. Worried about my upcoming speaking engagement, I asked the doctors if I could still travel that Friday via airplane. The doctor said, "Yes, as long as you take your anti-coagulant medicine, hydrate, and move around the cabin every hour." I went to Houston to speak. And the morning after I returned home, I had chest pain again with shortness of breath. I rushed into the ER to find out that I had a pulmonary embolism in my lung! I would then be hospitalized and treated with anti-coagulants for six months.

The first two weekends in November 2019, I went to a large speaker's conference and was a panelist at a women's retreat. Both were in Virginia. The chest pain when I breathe in and shortness of breath had come back with a vengeance! I found myself in the hospital over the Thanksgiving holiday and had a bronchoscopy done. It was inconclusive, and so I underwent a VATS lung biopsy while in the hospital over the New Year's holiday.

Speaking almost took my last breath! But what I have come to understand about life is that God transforms your test into a testimony, your mess into a message, and your misery into a ministry. I kept looking for "a diagnosis" and getting frustrated because oftentimes, things didn't make any sense. But what I also learned on the healing journey is that I am more resilient, more fearless, and more grateful than I ever was before! I could have died at any point in this experience, BUT God said, "No, it is not so!"

If you want to truly WIN in life, let me encourage you that get up whenever life knocks you down. A visionary writer from London, H.G. Wells said, "If you fell down yesterday, stand up today!" Inspire others with your story as often as possible. The great poet Maya Angelou said, "There is no greater agony than bearing an untold story inside of you." And finally, never give up on yourself, as long as you have breath in your body! Live on purpose.

Constance Craig-Mason

Constance Craig-Mason is the Visionary of Concierge Financial Group and CFG Agency. She is a passionate International Speaker, award-winning Insurance Broker, dedicated Financial Wellness Coach and a x3 Amazon Best Selling Author, who marries positive beliefs, emotions & daily money habits with financial literacy fostering a shift in her client's financial well-being! Constance empowers her clients to live the life they want without worrying about money!

She has received numerous awards for community impact in her field including a Medallion - "In Recognition of Excellence, Service, & Sacrifice" from the Comptroller of Maryland. Constance was an honoree at The Black Business Review's 2019 Class of 40 Under 40. She was nominated for Financial Expert Speaker of the Year at the SpeakerCon convention in November 2019. And Constance is a graduate of the 2020 Inaugural Class of Dr. Cheryl Wood's Vocalize Women Speakers Academy.

To connect go to www.ccraigmason.com.

The Power of a Woman of Change By Choice ©

By Doris DeeDee Cutler

A woman of change by choice sets out to discover her purpose. She is often driven to change because of the challenges in her life. It's usually when a woman of change gets tired of life's challenge and sets out to change the outcomes of her circumstances. Are you ready to become a woman of change by choice? Now, one can say she's going to change, but change will not take place until she believes change is taking place. "With God, all things are possible to those who believe." This also applies to the woman who decides she's ready to change and understands the choice is hers. This woman takes control of her destiny. She can't believe in something that she's not going to work towards making happen. A woman destined for change moves forward with her head held high and strength that cannot be denied. By her choice, she decides to forge the gaps that hold her in bondage, preventing her change by choice by her own forces.

I am an African American female, born in the mid-sixties, who grew up in the District of Columbia's inner city with a mother who could not read or write. According to the world's standards, she was considered illiterate. She did not complete grade school; could not read or write in complete sentences. Nevertheless, this amazingly confident black woman advocated for my educated and always assured me that I could be and do whatever I put my mind to. She was bursting with common sense and definitely one of the smartest women I knew. She exuded confidence, passion, and was persistent about always giving back and helping others. She could not read, but she spoke very well. She could hold conversations and others never know she could not read.

"A woman is like a tea bag. You never know how strong she is until she gets in hot water."
Eleanor Roosevelt

When I was about six years old, I came home from school excited to show my mother my book fair flyer and asked her to help me pick a book to buy. She slowly dropped her head, and she began to sob softly. I stood on the sofa to hug her and asked, "Mommy, why are you crying"? This was the first time I saw this remarkably unstoppable woman break-down into tears. I didn't understand and thought I did something wrong. I asked, what did I do to make you sad? With pronounced humiliation, she answered, "I can't read." Although I still did not really understand at that time, I said it's ok, angrily balled up the flyer up, and threw it in the trash. I returned to school the next day, and when the teacher asked who was going to the book fair. I angrily told her I was not going to the book fair because my mother could not read it.

A few weeks later, school ended, and I was chosen to attend the summer program. It wasn't until years later that I learned my first-grade teacher made sure I attended the summer program every year. She became my summer schoolteacher, and tutor. She assured my mother that someone would always work with me to make sure I stayed on task and that my homework was always completed. She also made sure every fall my new teachers were aware of my situation; the help would continue. It was because of my teacher that I learned to love reading. She inspired me to work hard and to strive to always do my best. My mother was my greatest cheerleader and encouraged me to read to her. By the time I was in middle school, I could read well enough; I had become my mother's reading translator. I graduated high school and went on to have a very successful career with the Metropolitan Police Department.

My first assignment was in a community where many youth were challenged in reading. Every encounter with the children reminded me of my first-grade teacher. In the field of law enforcement and the criminal justice system, these youth and young adults were often labeled as troubled or delinquents. When, in fact, they were smart and talented children who learned differently and just needed someone with the patience to help them. It was then I learned that the power of patience empowers! Many of these youth were struggling in school and had poor reading and math scores. It was painful to see them struggle, but it was even more painful to learn that they were struggling due to a lack of resources due to their communities' social and economic status. I began to volunteer with a small population of students in various schools within the community. This volunteer time fostered mentoring and tutoring relationships that increased reading scores and grades.

In 1995, I started Divine Images Network, a non-profit women's empowerment and image consultant group, to empower women to invest in themselves and their children's education. The organization promoted refinement and developed cultures to embrace higher education, established and cultivated family values, and strengthened community relationships. This project operated for more than 20 years in the community in which I worked. We encouraged and promoted the importance of education and its effects on the children, families, and community.

In 2012, my husband deployed to Afghanistan and was seriously injured. As a result of that incident, I had to leave the business to become his temporary full-time caregiver. I dissolved the organization at the end of 2015. During that time, I began to think about how choices are long lasting and life changing.

Life happened; I got married, became an army wife, worked a full-time job in law enforcement, had children, and became a part-time caregiver to my mother until she transitioned, started and worked my non-profit, and later became a temporary caregiver for my husband. "Hold up; I got lost somewhere in all this!

In the summer of 2013, I went back to school and finished my undergraduate degree in Criminal Justice. I was fifty-two years old when I graduated with my Bachelor's in Justice Administration and fifty-five when I graduated with my Masters in Homeland Security. It's never too late to change; the choice is yours.

"A woman with a voice is, by definition, a strong woman."
Melinda Gates

In 2020, amid a worldwide pandemic, the organization was relaunched as the Women of Change By Choice Movement ©, a network of women still promoting education with a refined focus on economic, social, and political empowerment for the future of women and girls. An image of confidence promotes success in every area of a woman's life. It doesn't matter who you are, what you've, or where you come from; the choice to change is yours! Change begins with a vision that's birthed from the very depths of one's soul. Effective change is a heart condition; so, take the WCCM pledge to "Become A Woman of Change by Choice" ©.

I chose to make substantial changes in my life for me, my children, and my children's children. The woman who decides to change by choice begins her legacy as she rips the runway that God designed just for her.

"If you want something said, ask a man; if you want something done, ask a woman."
Margaret Thatcher

The following stats are disturbing and unbelievable that in the 21st century, we still have such a high adult illiteracy rate.

United States Illiteracy (Gaille, 2017)

In the United States, the illiteracy rate has not changed in the past ten years. According to the US Department of Education and the National Institute of Literacy, the following statistics outline the state of literacy in the United States.

1. 32 million adults cannot read in the United States, equal to 14% of the population.

2. 21% of US adults read below the 5th-grade level.

3. 19% of high school graduates cannot read.

4. 85% of juveniles who interact with the juvenile court system are considered functionally illiterate.

5. 70% of inmates in America's prisons cannot read above the fourth-grade level.

Global Illiteracy (Gaille, 2017)

Illiteracy is not just confined to the borders of the United States. Worldwide, 774 million individuals cannot read. Unfortunately, 66% of this group of illiterates are female.

Many of these females are mothers who cannot help their children read, write, or do their homework.

Doris DeeDee Cutler

Doris D. Cutler is a visionary professional with a track record of success in nonprofit development and operational management. The former Law Enforcement Detective is well disciplined, self-motivated, and results-orientated with exceptional problem solving and time management skills. She is an entrepreneurial leader and exceptional communicator who interacts effectively with diverse populations.

As an accomplished Spokesperson and Gender Advocacy Thought Leader, she presents on women's empowerment, gender advocacy, sexual assault, domestic and family violence. She has served as a domestic violence advisor to the DC Commission for Women, a delegate to UN Gender Equity and Governance Conferences in the Americas, and Gender and Economic Development CIFAL Atlanta.

She holds a Bachelor of Arts in Justice Administration and Master of Science in Homeland Security with a concentration in Emergency Management from University of District of Columbia.

Contact DeeDee on all social media @deedeecutler4u or email: ddcutlerspeaks.com

His Healing Is Like Honey
By Shamika Dokes-Brown

Today, I can clearly see God's faithfulness in my life. But, when I was younger, it was difficult to see faithfulness, even though I believe in Him. See, I had a few obstacles along the way. My life had many twists and turns. Unaware of how to manage them, I chose to self-medicate with alcohol and marijuana, but I also did hair and dreamed of owning a hair salon. Running my own hair salon was my inspiration. I had even chosen the name, but unfortunately, this dream was placed on hold when I became pregnant at seventeen.

I can recall my first OB-GYN appointment during my senior year. I remember lying on the exam table looking at the monitor, watching this baby moving around inside of me but not feeling it. This is a lesson all on its own, because although you may not feel something, it doesn't mean it's not there. Tears began to roll down my cheeks, and it was in that moment; it became real.

Several things needed to be done before the baby arrived. I tried maintaining my hair clients, but morning sickness would sometimes last all day, and it wasn't easy to achieve much, but I tried. When I gave birth to my son, I had a lot of fear about being a mother. Although I had a great support system, the struggle between what I wanted and what God had for me began.

Being a mother was one challenge but dealing with postpartum depression was a whole other beast. This was nothing like the television show "A Baby Story," I would watch on TLC. I was overwhelmed, knowing this little person depended on me for everything. I wanted to give him the world - and everything I didn't have. It was my objective. But things started to worsen. When I think about the mood swings, it brings back many emotions. In the past, it was not fashionable to speak about postpartum depression. At the time, I did not even know the term, and clearly, no one recognized I was struggling, so I learned a different way to cope. I would have a shot of Hennessy in the morning to get me going, then hit the bottle, from time to time, throughout the day as a pick me up. I believed I was managing well, and that it was not affecting my parenting skills. I had a difficult time acknowledging that I had a drinking problem.

At 18, things worsen, and I found myself fighting a court case. The charges were justifiable, but at the time, it wasn't easy to see. I remember thinking something has to give. That's when I began reminiscing about my childhood. I was brought up "around" the church. My family belonged to the Church of God in Christ. I knew and believed that God was real despite the choices I had made. I would call my grandmother, "Big Mama," who stood 5 feet tall with high heels. I thought she had a direct line to heaven, so I would call her if I needed anything. I remember that while pregnant experiencing excruciating back pain. I called Big Mama on that lovely cordless phone with the metal antenna and asked her to pray for me. She went before the throne of grace on my behalf. It was like she pulled heaven down, asking the Lord to touch my body, and there was always a warmth that covered me when she prayed, and I felt assured that the Lord indeed heard her prayers.

I also remember attending Sunday service with my grandfather, "Big Daddy," at Holy Temple, our family church. Elder McCormick would preach on Sunday morning, as I sucked on green apple Jolly Ranchers from my uncle, L.C. I always looked forward to the service because I knew it would be good. My cousin-Gwen would play the organ, and I would watch from the pew. My other cousin, who we referred to as "Auntie Helen," would begin to sing "What More Can He Do," and then the entire congregation would join in. These were precious memories.

Although I knew something had to give at 18, it was not until I was 21 years old that things started to shift. We moved into our grandparents' home after we lost ours, and it was not easy. Living in this "super holy" environment, I could no longer drink the same, and hiding it was difficult. Instead, I limited my drinking and began smoking three packs of cigarettes a day. I used whatever means to compensate. I needed to make it through the day. At the time, my Aunt-Betty invited me to her church. I did not imagine joining, but we never know what God has planned for us. My sister and I had the address, but the GPS navigation was a little sketchy, so we got lost. As we searched, I remember opening my mouth to tell my sister, "let's give up." However, lo and behold, after crossing the railroad tracks, 1034 66th Ave, Oakland CA we arrived at the church. It was a real God moment. As we walked in, the Bishop's message was titled "Now Faith Is," the foundation scripture was Hebrews 11:1 NKV. "Now, faith is the substance of things hoped for, the evidence of things not seen." It was something about how the man of God would teach the Word that stirred up a hunger in me. I desired to learn more about the Word of GOD. I couldn't wait for Sunday morning or Wednesday night Bible study. I found a place of peace, and it was filling my "spiritual" gas tank.

Soon after, our congregation went on a 21-day consecration. A consecration is another term for fast, and this was my first time fasting. At the time, I was still smoking three packs of cigarettes a day. One Sunday, during the fast, something supernatural happened during worship service. I suddenly had an awareness of heaven that I had never experienced before. It was amazing, and I knew something had changed in me. Typically, after service, I would get in the car and have a cigarette. It had become a routine, but after this service, I remember getting in the car, and the desire to smoke was gone. I took the packs of cigarettes I had and crumbled them. With a smile on my face, I pushed the audiotape from service into the tape player. I was in love. There was a gentleness that I felt, and now, I didn't want to disappoint the LORD. Changes continued to happen; I intentionally cut off relationships that were unhealthy. Each day, it became clear God's presence was always with me. I was now learning to recognize it. As time went on, I fell deeper. I loved seeking God through His Word because I would get lost in it. I did not want this love affair to end. Another poignant moment occurred while I attended a women's retreat in Lake Tahoe, and we sang 'How He Loves' by David Crowder. It felt like the LORD had written this love letter directly to me.

"He is jealous for me, loves like a hurricane, I am a tree, bending beneath the weight of his wind and mercy..."

Those weren't just words sung over music; it was a part of the love story written about me by my heavenly Father. Those words covered my heart like honey, slowly dripping into the fragmented areas of disappointment, grief, unfulfilled dreams, and much more. We had what I call now a "daddy and daughter date," sitting next to the still water. I listened to the water crash upon the rocks as the sunray shone upon my face, and joy rested in my heart. I wanted nothing more but to never leave out of His presence.

Psalm 147:3, *"He heals the brokenhearted and binds up their wounds."*

Another awakening that this love wasn't a one-sided relationship. He didn't just start loving me. He loved me the entire time. As the Lord drew me closer, the easier it was to trace his hand in my life.

Shamika Dokes-Brown

Shamika Dokes-Brown is a resilient innovator. As Lena Mae's Bath and Beauty Boutique's owner, Shamika has pressed through barriers and boundaries to attain what others believed were insurmountable goals. This tenacity led to Lena Mae's birthing in the kitchen of her late mother. After her mother's death, she turned trauma, grief, and struggle into strength and determination. This fortitude was used to craft and produce her skin-loving products. For over 18 years, Shamika has remained committed to making a difference in Women's Health and Family Wellness.

Unveiled, Uncovered, Unfulfilled, And Unemployed: My Recovery Back To Faith

By Ursala A. Garnett

Unemployment, when spoken or heard, has a negative connotation, but more importantly, unemployment is more detrimental when you have to LIVE IT for three years.

Unemployment for me was no easy task. One month I could handle, six months I was prepared for, but three solid years was unimaginable, even in my own mind, and how would I survive. It was definitely a test of my faith and a test of my patience.

Unemployment was absolutely debilitating, exhausting, and infused with anger when in actuality, at times, I had times of great peace and sweet relief.

Living this life-changing ordeal was no walk in the park and definitely no "crystal stair". My journey began in April 2016 as a result of being overworked, undervalued, and not being paid my full worth when I was actually performing the role of two job descriptions but only receiving the income for one. This fiasco led me into a world of trouble physically and medically speaking. The stress of this role caused me to be diagnosed with Vestibular Migraines; at times, having to hold onto the wall to walk was difficult, and then it bloomed into having dizzy spells while driving to the point I nearly blacked out on the road. At this juncture of my life, many difficult decisions needed to be made, and I had to choose what was best for me and my life. The decisions were not easily determined. I spent much time in prayer, asking God what I should do. Patiently awaiting God's response to me, an answer was given right down to the last detail. I had the exact day I was to leave and knew what needed to be done. When the time came, I did not remain obedient to God's instructions only because I was trying to be a nice person and care about the people I worked for when in actuality, their feelings were not demonstrated equally. My date was April 15, 2016, I was to leave, and I gave them the benefit of the doubt and remained until April 22, 2016. What a mistake that was!

The real lesson of this entire story is never let anyone deter you from what you already know that God has spoken to your Spirit and never be disobedient when you're operating within a move of God. What comes to mind as I write, "You can please some people some of the time, but you can't please all people none of the time". And putting other people's needs before your own can be very costly and detrimental to your journey.

Being unemployed left me in a state of vulnerability and even to the point it felt like a death-a death of your goals, death of your dreams, and a death to your aspirations. To my family and friends, it was almost as if I had some contagious disease.

UNVEILED

Unemployment will change the dynamics of your relationships when you need to lean on and depend on those who love you and say they are your friends. Many times, it left me hurt and shameful. It destroyed me emotionally and caused me to go into depression. Unemployment definitely revealed who my friends were and who they were not. It also unveiled those who were sitting on the sidelines waiting for me to fall, to lose it all, just so they would have the opportunity to gloat and point fingers. A couple of them wanted to find out how I was able to stay in my house during all that time. Inquiring minds always want to know! Just know that God will send you some amazing friends who will never leave your side no matter what, and they will uplift you and tell you you have so much to live for. Proverbs 18:24 reads: "A man that hath friends must show himself friendly: and there is a friend that sticketh closer than a brother". I owe a gratitude of thanks to my two best friends, Randee and Marlyn. They kept me grounded and spoke life into me during my darkest place in my unemployment. And lastly, the impact unemployment had on me with future employers was insulting to unbelievable during my 3-year journey. Many of the things prospective employers asked were very insulting, some degrading, and others were unbelievable such as, "we need you to dumb down your experience to be suited for this role". Those kinds of things irritated the hell out of me, and I made up in my mind, "I ain't selling my soul to the devil today"! Period!

Key Point: "Never let ANYONE make you feel less than who you are."

UNCOVERED

While being unemployed, it put me in a predicament that I never knew I would face. It left me feeling exposed, naked, and on display for the world to see. Even though I knew there was greatness on the inside of me, I found it difficult to find through all the pain and the shame. I was so lost, confused, and searching for my purpose in life. This challenge alone was frustrating and draining. Little by little, my depression was getting deeper and deeper, and I found it difficult to grab hold of the faith I once stood on. After becoming unemployed, the goal was to open up my business and focus on my governance, risk, and compliance expertise. I took the necessary steps to get my business running, and then I got to a place where I was STUCK! So stuck, I felt paralyzed and began to doubt who and what I was. Everything started to go wrong. The savings I had put away started to dwindle after the first year and a half; then all hell broke loose in my life problem after problem took me lower and lower to the point I couldn't see my way clear. I spent many nights crying trying to find out what I was going to do, and right at that two-year mark of unemployment, every penny I had saved was gone. Here I am no income, no job, and no relief in sight. It's very hard to live with the truth when you are 51 years old and now having to depend upon your retired parents to keep you afloat. This was the most difficult thing I had to face, not to mention I was facing foreclosure of my home. During my three years of unemployment, I faced foreclosure three times. The stress was simply unbearable. As I looked back over my life, I realized that for years I had poured so much into others by helping them start and run their businesses that when the time came to run my own, I was burnt out and no support.

Key point: "Never pour more into other's dreams than your willing to pour into your own dreams". Remember, a good woman only gives from her bucket and never from her well. ~Ursala

UNFULFILLED

After living a time of being stuck and not discovering my purpose in life, I felt in my soul that I was unfulfilled. Always feeling that somewhere you've missed the mark. Never finishing what you started and residing in a place of fear that grips you that you make every attempt to get out of this rut, but it appears there's no way out. So, you look for ways that are not the conventional way, but a way that one should never entertain. Yes, things were so difficult; I thought of committing suicide three times because I believed it was my only way out, and this way, I would no longer be a burden to anyone. But just as that thought came for the very last time, I heard this voice that said, "Now what would that solve"? "Do you realize how many people you would impact by taking the easy way out?" "How would your parents deal with this?" And I literally cried out to God, please help me take away this pain that I feel. I'm here today to tell you it didn't happen overnight. It was definitely a process to get me back on the road to recovery. I had to reach deep down and be determined in my mind and heart that I needed to survive because one day, my story will have impacted a nation of people because of how I overcame unemployment and journeyed my way back to the faith I held so dear.

Key point: "Never entertain anything that does not serve you, your purpose, or your destiny." Ursala

UNEMPLOYED

I lost a lot during this time. I lost friends, the love of my life, and many loved ones along the way, but just when I had believed I had lost my faith, there it was waiting for my return.

I thank God for my parents, who stood by me, and God, who never left me.

THE END!

Ursala A. Garnett

Uncovered: "Living with the truth, you're 51 years old, unemployed, and depending upon your retired parents to keep afloat."

Ursala A. Garnett, a spiritually motivated, charged woman, is a Chief Consultant, expert in governance, risk, and compliance for GRC Consulting Group, and first-time published author.

Many of Ursala's personal writings have been inspired from her time in prayer and communion with God. Her writings are based on her life's challenges and situations that have shaped her life.

Ursala contributed one of her writings to Christian Poets and Writers entitled "The Elephant In the Room".

Being a survivor of unemployment is a fete. The life challenges one has to face can be an unpleasant experience in one's life. It's good to have a solid foundation, loving support, and faith and determination to break through.

Ursala can be reached at: ursala_garnett@yahoo.com, https://www.facebook.com/ursala.garnett, https://www.Instagram.com/ursala777, and ursalagarnett777@gmail.com

A Successful Failure
By Tanika T. Garrett

It's fine to celebrate success but it is more important to heed the lessons of failure.
- Bill Gates

Have you ever felt so low in your life that you start to question your ability, calling, and skills? I can almost guarantee you have. Don't fret; there is an answer. In my life, I have experienced some failures and felt so low that I questioned myself too. But there's this one particular time that I almost threw in the towel and said forget it all. Although I didn't quite see the way out as I was going through this test, I had to stay the course to discover my answer(s).

"Well, what's the test?" you may ask. I'm going to share it with you. But first, let's define what a failure is. According to Merriam-Webster Dictionary(2020), failure is an omission of occurrence or performance; a state of inability to perform a normal function. Me? A failure? Not normal? No way! At least that was my initial reaction. Let's take a look at this scenario, which captures a memorable moment of a successful failure.

"Mommy!" the little girl called. "I have to interview you, remember."

"Yes, I remember," said Mommy. "I'm ready. What do you have to ask me?"

"I only have one question. Have you ever failed at something?"

"Why, yes. Yes, I have. I'll explain. You know Mommy is a teacher, right?"

"Right."

"So, I had to take this test in order for me to continue teaching."

"Continue teaching?" the little girl emphasized.

"Yes! I had already taught a few years prior, but in order for me to continue doing so, I had to take some other classes and take a test called the Praxis®. You see, the Praxis tests measure the academic skills and subject-specific content knowledge needed for teaching (The Praxis® Tests, n.d.). It's a required part of receiving certification in my state. The first time I took the test, I really didn't think I needed to study (practice) as much because I was taking upper-level courses already. Wrong! I failed. Next, I retook the test, and I studied alone. I failed. Following, I paid for the test but failed to appear to take it. That was an automatic failure. I took it yet again- failed. Again, here I was, but this time I prepared with a tutor, meaning I had someone to help me study (practice). And guess what? I failed. Ugh! The frustration, wasted money, time, energy was overwhelming to me. I talked with several people at this point. But, I had a conversation with my mom, and she shared with me to start reading Psalm 34 and 37 every day. I did just that. Not only that, but others needed help as well. So, we formed a study group. We would meet after class or any time we had in between to meet and practice. After this attempt, with much preparation, praying, and reading, I finally passed. I had registered for this test seven times, paid for it seven times, took it five to six times, and finally passed."

"Oh, my goodness! That's a lot of times." the little girl sat flabbergasted.

"Yes, but I didn't give up. It's much like when you didn't do well on your test. You realized that you had not prepared for it. But, now you know the material because you went back and practiced more."

"You're right. I remember," the little girl recalled gazing up towards the sky.

"Although this was a physical test that I needed to pass, there are, have been, and will be more situations that test us. But, with that, there are things we learn from them."

"You're right, Mommy. I'm glad you didn't give up."

"Thank you! And I know you won't either. I see it in you even now. Is that enough information for your interview?"

"Yes, it is. Thank you, Mommy!"

Now, although this story was dramatized to demonstrate a lesson to the little girl about not giving up after a failure, it's a true one. This was me from 2008 to 2010. Although this was a physical test I needed to pass, there are, have been, and will be more situations that test me. But now I have some experience with the feelings of what it can bring. In addition, while I was trying to pass this test, I tried to do it on my own strength. I neglected to consult, if you will, the Creator of me. Not that I'm not a woman of faith, but I failed to include God. How many times have you gotten so enthralled with something that you didn't have a conversation (pray) with God for guidance, direction, or permission?

I'm reminded of David in the Bible. He wanted to move the Ark of the Covenant. When he and his men did move it by cart, a man named

Uzzah died. He did because he put his hands out to catch the Ark of the Covenant, which he didn't have permission to do. David did not follow through with the law of that time. It was the Levites' job to carry it, not for it to be on a wagon cart. After this, David asked what to do, and the next trip was successful. So, you see, with God, all things are possible. It wasn't that David wasn't trying to please God. Quite the contrary. He just went about it the wrong way. And that was the same with me. I knew I had deadlines to meet. But my approach was wrong. That's what failing will do- teach you lessons. And in the fail are lessons for me to learn more about myself. Here I was wanting to teach, but, yet again, I failed at being the student. It wasn't my time yet. There was more for me to learn as a student. Don't misunderstand me. We are all life-long learners. Now, I purposely look for lessons in my failures and self- reflect on what to do differently.

Countless others have successful failure stories. A few include Bill Gates of the Microsoft Corporation., Colonel Sanders of Kentucky Fried Chicken (KFC), Jack Canfield, author of Chicken Soup for the Soul books, and Mary Kay Ash of Mary Kay Cosmetics.

So, what now? How do you bounce back after a failure? I would like to suggest the following to help you:

1. **Acknowledge it.** Admit where you messed up. Look for the next opportunity to fix it.

2. **Take what you did and revamp it.** Take what didn't work and change the plan. I'll give you a hint: it's best to ask for help and/or feedback.

3. **Try again**. Celebrate that- trying again. Not all things are easy to attain. Exhaust all of your options.

4. **Don't forget your why.** Remember why you're going back to it. It's bigger than you. Someone is waiting on you to share what you have-gifts, skills, talents, and abilities to help propel them forward too.

Think about this. What if the failure were to produce fruit in you, and in turn, helps others do the same? It may sound like an oxymoron, but let's see. Don't throw away the failure; repurpose it and find its "new fruit." I'm sure you've heard or even said that "failure is not an option." It may not be an option, but it is going to happen. Failure doesn't have to be the end result. But, let it help build your way to greatness.

With my failure came darkness, uncertainty, feeling alone, and no ease. There were also glimpses of light, development, being built up for something greater than I, collaboration and more! My resiliency is because I failed. My strength is because I failed. There were lessons I needed to learn, an opportunity to grow and become better so that my success is on a greater scale. I found success in my failure.

As I close, I want to leave you with a portion of the lyrics from "I'm Still Standing":

I'm still standing
I'm still trusting
I'm still holding on to what I believe
Still motivated
Fully persuaded
I'm still standing
Standing on the word
On the word that's in my heart

References:

Carr, K. (2006). I'm Still Standing [Lyrics]. Retrieved from https://genius.com/Bishop-paul-s-morton-im-still-standing-lyrics

Failure (2020). https://www.merriam-webster.com/dictionary/failure

The Praxis® Tests (n.d.). Retrieved from https://www.ets.org/praxis

Tanika T. Garrett

Being a middle and high school Mathematics teacher with nearly 15 years' experience, Tanika's ability to build rapport is impeccable and values the growth of individuals while in her presence. She serves on various committees, all while being a lead teacher. She has received several accolades with the latest being awarded Peer Leadership Teacher of the Year for the 2018-2019.

Aside from teaching, Tanika is also the founder of Master in M.E.(My Existence), which holds a two-fold message. Individuals are able to master themselves and while having a relationship with the Master (God) know that they can fulfill their purpose. In addition, she is the author of Getting My Masters in M. E.- An Educator's Guide for Personal Development to Become More Impactful Professionally.

She is married to J. Andre' Garrett with two daughters and currently resides in central Alabama.

Connect: www.tanikagarrett.com | FB: Tanika Garrett

I Am Here

By Rochelle V. Gray

How did I GET here? How did I get HERE?

First, "here:" I am divorced! Lord, Lord, Lord... The second "here:"
I'm in Charlotte, North Carolina; 647 miles from New Jersey, where I
was born and raised... The final "here" is healed, where I am today.

Let me tell you a story...

It starts with the telling of my first "here." I am divorced: after 24
years of being with one man. I am blessed to have two beautiful
daughters, my sweet and logical firstborn: Antonaia and my ride or die,
lastborn: Caitlin. Man, let me tell you. I don't know when everything
started to unravel but unravel it did. Now, my ex-husband (you know
his name) was a "good guy." I'd be the first to tell anyone that. He just
"bumped his head." as I call it. Now, I know, I know... I'm not a
perfect person, and I wasn't the perfect wife; HOWEVER, I was still
willing to keep fighting. I did love him, and the thought of my family
being crushed was not something that I wanted to experience. What
about my daughters? How will this affect them? What about God?
What is He going to say? What is my church going to think? My
friends? Will I lose some? I'm no longer going to be a part of a couple.
I, a divorcee? I couldn't think! Now, I am determined to tell this story
from a real place and in a REAL way. I know that my words will hold
some surprises and revelations. Yeah, yeah, I know... different stories

have different perspectives… This is mine… life for the last 12 years…

I had a near-perfect life: a real strong relationship with God, a handsome husband, two beautiful daughters, attended a wonderful church, where I served on the choir and the praise team, as well as directing the Children's Choir, was working as an educator, which I loved (making close to 90 thousand dollars a year) and was serving as an elected official on the Highland Park Board of Education in New Jersey. I had really great friends and a wonderful extended family, especially on my ex-husband's side. I was SET!! Yeah right…

I didn't see the divorce coming. However, I knew that my marriage was in trouble about three years before we separated. Even before that, there were probably signs. I just couldn't imagine that we would not always be together, so I just ignored the signs. He wouldn't ever leave his family. Hmmm. I remember that when I first left the corporate world and started my journey to becoming an educator, it was my ex-husband's idea. He encouraged me to begin the journey to becoming who I really was purposed to be, an educator. We talked about decisions that would affect our family. I saw him as the priest of my home and always (so I thought) ran things by him. So, when I got my B.A., we were in agreement. We talked about it. Then after I graduated, I encouraged him. He got his degree, and I was happy for him! Some years later, I decided to enter a master's program, so I consulted with my ex-husband. To this day, I hear his words at the conclusion of the conversation: "Are you saying that I can't take care of you?" DING! DING! DING! What??!!!! My response was that most educators want to become a "master" at their craft. Hindsight is 2020. Did I miss something? Did HE agree, or did he AGREE with ME?

Long story short, I received my masters. We had our first child, Antonaia, and eventually bought a home. I was living a great life. We traveled two or three times a year. I took care of our children, and my ex-husband took care of us.

Next missed sign... My ex-husband started to resign from key positions in our church in Montclair... Hmmm. What was that about?. We had been commuting from Highland Park to Montclair for several years, so we (no I) began to look for another church for our family. Hmmmm. As I reflect as I am writing this, I remember that I began not to want my husband's advances. I know that this made him angry, frustrated, and disappointed. However, something was off, and I couldn't put my finger on it. Real talk, having sex was starting to hurt. Reflection, the "be(fore)play wasn't like it had been at the beginning of our marriage. However, we had been married for close to 20 years, so I thought the problem was with me. My doctor couldn't find anything wrong. However, I just kept feeling that something was "off." My ex-husband had started a new position and I know that a lot of "stuff" was going on down there. One of my friends likened it to "Sodom and Gomorrah." On one occasion, I asked him if some of my friends and I needed to "come through there." So, I had some signs. Now, let me say, I am not saying that I am blameless. Our sex life was going downhill. I couldn't understand why it hurts to have sex with my husband, and the occasions became fewer and fewer. I was determined to find out the problem. Again, I know that my ex was hurting too.

I noticed that my ex started "working out a lot." He's not bothering me about sex, and I'm just going about doing my other duties. Remember the song, "This is the Beginning of My End," by The Unifics (2008). I decided to check out a doctorate program in Texas. While I was preparing to return home, my youngest daughter called and said, "Mom, Dad just bought a BMW Convertible, he has put his earring back in his ear, and he has his Kangol hat on backward." My world crashed. Although we had discussed me getting my doctorate, the conversation wasn't that long, more like an. "OK." Conversation over!. My first thought was, "can men go through the change? I hurried home. The conversation was bleak. He described his unhappiness, and we decided to go for marriage counseling. Now, some years later, I thought about our decision and its timing. I think that my ex had already moved on and was just playing the role. We set up counseling appointments at our church, and he canceled all three. No one really knew what I was going through.

We found a new counselor. Well, our church referred us to a woman who, although she was a born-again believer, she didn't run her practice biblically, and she told us so. Hmmmmm. SET UP! RUN! I thought. However, I was too scared that my husband wouldn't go to counseling at all.

Revelation. After four sessions, the counselor made a separate appointment with me and said, I don't usually tell my clients this; however, get ready. Your husband doesn't want to be married to you. Every issue that he brings up as a reason to not go on is something that can be solved easily. Also, I had brought up the idea for me to go to a specialist about my problem having pain during sex. My husband said, no, that's not necessary. We were both hurting... So, I thought... Maybe in different ways.

One day my "husband" told me that he is taking a weekend trip and that he would decide whether to stay in the marriage or leave. At this time, I just wanted closure. He returned. He had decided to leave. I coldly responded, "Pick a day.' We went downstairs and spoke with our daughters. It was so painful, remembering their reactions. Their father asked which of us did they want to live with, and they piped up, " Mommy!" My ex had tears rolling. I was just numb. We were going to be separated. I'm thinking, "maybe he'll eventually miss us and come home."

January 4th -He moves out. January 12th - I fall on black ice and break my ankle. The break is so bad that I am out of work from January until May!! I saw my ex-husband two times. We moved to Piscataway, where I worked. God provided a way for us. However, I had to give up my seat on the Board of Education because I no longer resided in that city. I was in my third term. I really felt the loss.

We needed a change of scenery. My dad suggested that we move to Charlotte, N.C. What??

However, what did we have to lose? It turns out that God was truly with us. We moved to Charlotte. We've met some wonderful people who helped us heal. My daughter Caitlin really thrives here. My purpose is being fulfilled. I'm even ready for a relationship! My final "here" is being healed and ready, for I know that the best IS yet to come!

Rochelle V. Gray

Rochelle V. Gray is an educator with twenty-two years' experience, who is currently with the Charlotte Mecklenburg school system. She received her B.A. from Kean University in Public Administration and her M.Ed. from Fairleigh Dickinson University in Educational Leadership. In addition, she was elected to three terms with the Highland Park Board of Education in New Jersey.

In 2019, her non-conventional sports, entrepreneurship, and leadership program, "Empower the Youth", along with her great advocacy of youth, earned her Gen One's teacher of the year.

When she isn't advocating for students, she spends time writing, singing, crocheting, and playing chess. She is currently developing an educational program for Black and Brown males in the K-12 school setting, and a training company for aspiring and new teachers named, "Vision Over Sight".

She presently resides in Charlotte, North Carolina with her daughter Caitlin.

She can be reached at info@visionoversight.com or http://www.visionoversight.com/

A Fearless Woman...
By Cherie Griffith-Dunn

I told myself that she didn't have to die like this… She was a knockout. "Boy, oh, boy!" She was one who was envied by all with her long black wavy hair, hourglass shape, perfect breast size, and distinct look – a cross between a Native Indian and a White woman.

The looks she would get whenever we went anywhere made me unsure if they were for how beautiful she was or why she had black children with her. My father was a darker Black man, so most of us came out this weird yellow color. I remember being about five years old and asking my mother why she would lay in the sun in our backyard. She smiled and told me to come close, so I did, and she whispered, "because people will respect me more when I'm darker." I grew up with that thought in my head and found myself being looked at the same way when tanning in the back yard, never thinking anything more of it. I figured the apple does not fall far from the tree.

My mother was one of the nicest people I knew in my life. She was kind, gentle, loving with a calming smile that would light up the room and make you feel loved. No matter who she met, the old man down the street who was mean to us, the man who stayed behind the Caldor's, or the woman who never had enough to eat or anyone to watch her children; she made everyone feel worthy and loved.

My mother had a reputation of always helping those who I thought should not be helped; you know, so and so's son who was a drug addict, the old man who drank too much and was known for peeing on himself, the misunderstood man who had a job but couldn't keep his hands off his wife, and even the girl who ran away because her mother's boyfriend raped her. She would say, "these people are just down on their luck, baby, and a little love with a hot meal could be what they need to change their circumstance." Plus, she believed that the world takes care of you and yours when you give back to it. She would frequently say, "I would never want one of you girls to be in the streets alone needing a smile and warm food in your belly, no matter what you did; besides, people will always remember how you made them feel, and sometimes that's all they need."

Fast forward to the day it all started to spiral downhill. There must be something said for what loneliness can do to someone's state of mind. How it can bring you off the top of the mountain into the lowest valley. My mother had begun to lose everything she held dear to her, her family. She was not prepared for that day, the day your kids go off to college and never return. That day you wake up and never see the man you poured your life into, your knight in shining armor lying beside you, that day, when your kids grow up and discover their own life. Little do you realize how that sadness affects everyone around you for years; it lays a dark cloud around those attached to you. The persistent feeling of sadness or loss of interest that embodies major depression can lead to a range of behavioral and physical symptoms. These changes for my mother came in the form of alcohol and low self-esteem. It hurt so bad to watch this beautiful woman become the life she tried to save people from.

Though she was still kind, her beauty never slipped away, but she started to hide in shame from her family about what had become of her life. It seemed like, at times, she was happier with those who were suffering from the same form of self-sabotage. Why is it when we make a mistake, we tend to wallow in it for what seems like forever, forgetting about your loved ones and become consumed by darkness. What is the saying, you become like the five people you hang around? I had not realized that this had become her life, one that she was accustomed to, watching people suffer from being knocked down over and over again and then finding it difficult to get back up again. I guess her knockdown felt right at home, but she didn't realize that she wasn't taught the hard knocks game, so there were things she didn't know about that life.

As time went on, her kindness became mistaken for weakness. Those people who she felt so compassionate about helping turned on her.

I will never forget the day I received the call, the call no one wants to receive, but you know the ring. It wakes you up out of sound sleep and has you shaken and frightened to your core. Yes, that ring. I picked up the phone shaking, and the lady on the other end told me to get to the hospital, "your mother had a bad accident, and she is dying." I dropped the phone, my heart was in my stomach, and I fell to my knees, screaming, "Father almighty, please do not take my mother from me; she's a good person." What I did not mention was that my mom had become my best friend after college. We spoke on the phone every day about everything and everybody. She seemed to be happy and had accepted her life for what it was; although I disagreed with it, I respected her and wanted to show her love.

To be honest, I do not remember how I got to the hospital or who had my two toddlers and newborn. All I remember is my husband holding me to walk, the smell of bleach and blood, and seeing my mother lying in that bed. It stills brings tears to my eyes when I talk about it. I rushed over to her to tell her that everything would be okay when the doctor said she did not make it. I was confused. "What do you mean," I asked. I was feeling her warmth. The doctor shook his head and walked out. I began screaming, "Mommy, wake up! Mommy, wake up!" I remember lying in bed with her for what seemed like hours until my husband said, let's go. That day marked the darkest day of my life.

My mother was murdered, and we still do not know who could have hit her in the head so hard that it would kill her.

Weeks went by, and I found myself not functioning. My milk almost dried up because I was not eating. I did not quite understand what was wrong with me or when I would feel normal again. My husband came home, and I was in my usual place with the kids in my bed. He said, "Cherie, we need to talk." There was that feeling again; something tragic was about to happen. I thought he would leave me or send me away or take my babies from me worse. As my heart pounded a million beats per second, he grabbed my hands and said, "I love you too much to see you suffer like this, so I took time off work to help you get better" This was the first time I could relate to how my mother must have felt all of these years, depressed, sad and stuck simply needing someone to care for her and make decisions to help her.

The next day I woke up determined to get help because I had people depending on me. I treated my post-traumatic stress syndrome and depression by going to therapy, praying every day, eating right, exercising, and no medication. This allowed me to continue breastfeeding my newborn and take care of my family, who needed me. I vowed to give back, so my life's work is now about helping others see their greatness and achieve their goals because life is not promised.

"Bless the Lord, oh my soul, and forget not all His benefits: who forgives all your iniquities, who heals all your diseases, who redeems your life from destruction, who crowns you with loving kindness and tender mercies, who satisfies your mouth with good things, so that your youth is renewed like the eagle's
(Psalm 103:2-5 NKJV).

Cherie Griffith-Dunn

Cherie Griffith-Dunn is a globally recognized motivational speaker, transformational catalyst coach, and author who uses her 7 E.L.E.V.A.T.E Your Life Principles to up level leaders. Her bold no nonsense business strategies have helped thousands of small business owners, entrepreneurs, and professionals achieve explosive growth and increase their income. As a transformational catalyst, Griffith-Dunn coaches small business owners, entrepreneurs, and professionals in up leveling their authority, getting noticed, growing their profitability, and separating themselves as a top leader in their industry. She has spent the last decade in leadership roles in Corporate America, developing rising leaders. Her audiences walk away with many skills, tools, and keys to mastering your millionaire mindset, bringing your genius to the next level, and owning your seat at the table. She and her business have been featured in 40 Under 40, Hartford Journal and Hartford Young Professional Entrepreneurs to name a few.

Finding Joy On The Journey, While Weathering The Storms
By Von M. Griggs-Laws

A decent and adventurous childhood in St. Louis, Missouri, consisted of both parents and four siblings. Storms raged early during my adolescent years. Our home was the "house party" on the block. Almost anyone could get help from the Griggs,' be they family, neighbors, or someone referenced to have fallen on a hard time. Parties started Thursday's nights, card parties, fish-fries on Fridays, and BBQ's plates sold on Saturdays. We didn't 'lack much of anything, well, except consistent peace & safety. My father worked very hard, a City of St. Louis employee, and always was a serial entrepreneur.

Storms raged when alcohol won over his senses & behavior. Violence were weekend occurrences. Family members told my mother, "he's your husband," you have to stay. My books and dolls offered me a place of joy & vowed to find a way out of those storms. Working since age 16, I soon followed my youngest brother's move and joined the military. I was impressed by the five digits on his US treasury check issued on the first and fifteenth of the month; free uniforms, food, benefits, and travel. It wasn't long that I gained respect and support from my parents.

The Air Force was my branch of choice, as the recruiter told me it was the most favorable of women. I wanted to march in the USAF Band because they wore the same royal blue colors as my high school, and I admired the flight caps. The recruiter lied to me. My first four years were in logistics, and the closest I got to the marching band was the Color and Honor Guards, which were both very rewarding and joyous. Those special duty details got me out of work, so I volunteered as often as possible. I was becoming accustomed to traveling, meeting people from all over the world, learning about other cultures and beliefs. That was all so exciting to me and was a major factor in my re-enlistment.

It had been only ten years or so; the Armed Forces had changed family policies on the premise that woman's responsibilities as wives and mothers took precedence over their military careers. Women were no longer involuntarily discharged for pregnancy. We could marry and equally receive military housing for families, medical care routinely available to servicemen's wives. Many older and younger generations were not embracing those changes. That was a storm of discrimination by both men, who felt women should not serve and the women who were intimidated by the fact that we were. I became accustomed to being the only person in the room who looked like me. I saw this as opportunities to represent and gain respect. I was grateful for every opportunity given and never wanted to be an embarrassment to myself, my parents, my country.

A short marriage was my next storm, catastrophic as a category four hurricane, with two amazing daughters, I divorced after seven years. Becoming a single parent while serving in Germany bought on a lot of growth. It was nine years before I returned to St. Louis to visit. I had learned and endured so much. I was immediately able to notice my growth and resilience, yet, most importantly, my values had also changed. Safety & security had become priorities. Most challenging were the many site inspections and deployments, having to leave my children. I learned to trust God even more. Desert Shield & Desert Storm were the longest separations. God was so faithful; Psalms 91 helped me through that war and the transition from combat and kept me from total fear.

Stormy situations I prayed and hope will pass, leave no sign that there was even a slight sprinkle of rain. During the nineties, more women enlisted in all branches of the services in droves. However, women in the military were thought of by some men as signing a sexual assault/harassment contract. I'm grateful that behavior was not constant, yet it was present. It took a lot of self-care, self-motivation, and self-esteem, not to become vulnerable. One mistake could tarnish your career. I say "mistake" in quotation marks because that "mistake" could be reporting a sexual assault that actually happens. Thank God, times have changed. So have the legal policies and laws, but unfortunately, there are still too many sexual assaults across gender equal to behaviors in corporate America. As a whole, the military has gotten better, yet there is still so much to be done.

These efforts helped change the combat exclusion ban on women in direct ground combat. They ushered in the opening of all positions for women in the armed forces.

No longer are the times where females' contributions tend to be ignored in favor of legacies left by men who have shaped the narrative of service to our country. Despite being overlooked, servicewomen are forging new career paths for themselves and the next generation as they enter jobs that were once closed to them. There are so many acknowledgments now of "she is the first..." I'm happy for all of their achievements!

While enlisted, there was a very long storm that raged for me during the fall season every year, called WAPS tests. For years, I carried humiliation and embarrassment for the inability to score high enough for promotion. One year, the storm hit like a category 10. I had been informed by headquarters that I had passed. I was literally at alterations having my new stripes sewn on my uniforms when I got a call on my radio to return to the office. I drove the jeep casually, not in a hurry, and the closer I got, the more nervous I was feeling. When I got to my Colonel's office, the Squadron Commander was there too. I saluted and asked. "Sir, are my children, okay?" He answered yes, My parent's okay? Again, a yes. Then he told me I had missed the mark by 0.96, not even a whole point.

The flood gates of that storm crashed so hard. It had been four days since the original promotion notifications. I had already experienced celebrations and congratulations from hundreds of people, from stateside and abroad. I muddled through months of appeals that were useless. That storm left years of residual damage and residue. The closer autumn came, the harder it was for me to have faith in myself. I was trusting God, yet there were many times I felt unfulfilled. I was living as righteousness as I knew how. I had received my ministry ordination, prayed, fasted, and often prayed for people that surpassed me. Those were true character-building years for me. I knew God was able, though, that was not the destiny He had for me. He trusted me with integrity to help others achieve what I thought I deserved. I was so happy to see His faithfulness. I found joy by using the skills I had. I became a well-renowned hair braider and was commissioned to teach ethnic hair care at a university in the United Kingdom. My side hustle allowed me to purchase my first home in a foreign country. In 2019, newly appointed CMSgt. of the Air Force, Kaleth Wright said leadership is eliminating Weighted Airman Promotion System, WAPS.

Remembering the Tuskegee Airman, who believed change would come related to segregation and discrimination, and Women Air Corps members that were discharged after WW11, and all the trailblazers that have gone before us and paved roads for African Americans and women to follow. The civilian women were able to work shoulder to shoulder with men in factories, on airfields, on farms, as shipbuilder's aircraft & ammunition manufacturers, bus, and streetcars operators, due to the war. And for that, I was so grateful.

Retirement ushered another storm. Grief, loss, and separation from what I had known, day in and day out for 20 years, was very hard. This next mission was unscripted and led to post-traumatic growth. There were no programs in place as now to fully assist with separating or discharging. Transitioning from that identity bought anxiety, nervousness, and expectations of the unknown. My coping mechanisms changed, devotion, and gratefulness grew. Many years later, I related to depression, from having learned to suppress my emotions and often my opinions and concerns. After moving to Texas, I enlisted in the State Guard, becoming the first Air Force African-American female to attend the Army's Officer Candidate School at Camp Mabry, TX, receiving the rank of 2nd. Lieutenant. That fourteen-year storm and all the aftermath was now gone. Along with self-esteem and emotional intelligence, my joy was being restored.

Know that occasionally a storm will stir. Life's situations can bring swift storms and slow-moving occurrences. They will cause the winds to pick up and the clouds to hang low. There may be days of overcast, with no sun. I pray that you will exercise gratitude and find joy on the journey!

Von M. Griggs-Laws

Von M. Griggs-Laws, born and raised in St. Louis, MO; served 26 years in the US Air Force and Texas State Guard. She is a graduate of the University of Maryland with a degree in psychology. Owner and inspirational sought-after trainer and coach in occupational safety & health at Griggs Safety Consultants, LLC. Von is an ordained minister & founder of Joy Restored Outreach, LLC, advocate for homeless female Veterans. She currently lives in Dallas, TX. with her husband Maurice Laws; they are blended parents to ten adult children & proud grandparents of five.

Featured talks:
The Essentials of Safety & Health/ Preserving Life & Limb
Your Joy Can Be Restored
You Are Not What Happened to You

Coming to the Stage
By Duania Hall

"She must've done something...no man is going to just randomly do that."
"You must've known this was going to happen."
"No one is going to want you with all those scars on your body."
"Girl...ain't you got no self-respect at all?"

***

I was fierce like the phenomenal woman Maya Angelou wrote about. Some knew me as their ride-or-die friend who always made them laugh or feel lifted during hard times. I was an active leader at church. I spent mornings driving from my two-bedroom townhouse to work at USC Hospital, where I was thriving. I spent nights hanging with my longtime boyfriend and dreaming about all I wanted for the future. Over time, my relationship had become unhealthy, and when I chose to end it, his response was nothing anyone could have prepared me for. I got accustomed to answering questions by the police, doctors, and lawyers. Now, nearly two years later, I finally was ready to talk about what happened to me.

***

My head was spinning with the echoes of comments from people who judged me because of my trauma. Their voices were so loud! It felt as if they were in the room with me, pressing in on me from every direction. Then, just as my head was about to go into overload and malfunction, I heard the host introduce me: "Coming to the stage we have this dope Sista. She came through before and did her thing. She's here to bless the mic again. Y'all show some love for Duania!"

The enthusiastic clapping of the audience drew me to them, almost against my will. Deep breaths in and deep breaths out, wiping away tears, then a quick pep talk; no turning back now. It was time to tell my own story, time to reclaim myself. The quicksand of fear that previously restricted my feet was finally loosening. There was no time to entertain the voices, or, as my therapist would say, the "old recordings," that so often disrupted my train of thought and derailed my peace. At last, it was time to come to the stage.

I was almost there. Now stepping into the spotlight, I turned around for just a moment to say goodbye to the shame that previously tried to silence me. I stepped to the mic with a boldness that surprised even me. I began: "How y'all doing?" I was feeling a little Erykah Badu-ish, so I followed up with, "Sistas, how y'all feeling? Brothas, y'all alright?" Except, instead of telling somebody to call Tyrone, I was sharing how my deliverance came when I relied on The One who sits on the Heavenly throne.

I began sharing my poetic testimony, and it was as if a lightning bolt of power ran through me! I was fired up! The question of how did this happen to me at this age shifted to what is my purpose here on this stage? Purpose! That was it! That was everything! At that moment, I knew my story had a purpose, and this was the beginning of its fulfillment.

Instead of depression and pain holding me hostage in the darkness, I was surrounded by light. The lights on the stage, the lights in the room, the light in the eyes of the people in the audience who held onto every word, and even the light in the tears of those whose hearts felt the beat of God's rhythm as I described how He delivered me from the snare of the fowler.

After I barred all of me in a room full of strangers, an unfamiliar man approached me: "That was so powerful, my Sista! Did that really happen to you?" Initially, I was thrown by his question, but I, however, quickly realized how hard it must be for him to imagine how this woman, standing before him looking like a fresh-baked peach cobbler with two scoops of vanilla ice cream and a spirit shining like the North Star, could have been through so much hell. So, I humbly responded, "Yes, that's my story. That's my testimony."

***

Often, the responses of others to our trauma breeds shame. I know now that I do not have to be ashamed of what I have been through. I no longer allow ill-informed opinions or expectations to devalue my experiences or who I am in Christ. This is my desire for you that you, too, will learn to embrace your whole journey and stop apologizing for who you are and the wisdom you have earned through your pain.

DO NOT ACCEPT THE LABEL OF SHAME!

Some people demand that survivors remain silent, so their piercing words won't disrupt their comfort. This allows them to avoid looking deeper at the problem or their role in the problem, denying the survivor the necessary space and support to achieve total healing.

My desire for wholeness ignites me to share my story unapologetically and to publicly glorify God for my deliverance. I want you to know that your story matters and some people want, no, need to hear it. Do not be ashamed to tell it! You are still who God says you are! You have a great purpose to fulfill on this earth. So, focus on Psalm 139:14, which says you are fearfully and wonderfully made. I leave you with the poem I shared the night I finally had the courage to tell my story:

RESURRECTION

Kitchen floor
In a pool of my own blood I was lying
As my man repeatedly stabbed me
I could feel that I was dying
And no one was around to hear me crying
Except for The One who hears the faintest plea
I called Jesus, who I knew could deliver me

At that moment I positioned my faith
So, my life could get an extension too
You are looking at the Mona Lisa
Of what God will do

I had stabs in my back and stabs in my arms
Devil looked on with pride
As his advocate did me harm
Stabs in my stomach and stabs in my legs
No begging for my life, God was already ahead

One more stab, now in the neck
Devil high-fived his 'peeps'
Cause my life he thought he wrecked
He must've forgot that Jesus died on the cross to set up my resurrect,
And in that very moment, it began to take effect

After that battle, I had emotional and physical scars
The devil thought he destroyed me
But he just raised the bar
Soon and very soon
All will know the reason I was created
Success is belated
But it's on time, 'cause it's God-dated

After that battle, I had 22 stabs

The devil thought my destiny was up for grabs
Malcom X said it best devil
"you've been bamboozled, hoodwinked,
had and led astray"
God decreed my tomorrow
So, you can't rob me of today

You lost the battle before you even got started
This thing between me and Jesus cannot be departed
You lost because you brought a boy
And I came back with The Man
Jesus sho-nuf had back up and a plan
He brought the angels, who are always down to ride,
They said "Look here devil, you can
torture her, but SHE WILL NOT DIE!"

That was my resurrection
Now I want you to take a moment of
Recollection of His reflection and
The devil's perplexion
Every time Jesus provides you with protection
I say this with affection

Jesus died on the cross
So, you could salvage your life's pieces
Under His love's perfection and
Not be restrained by sin's subjection

New breath in my body came down from Heaven
I'm not the same little girl, but a woman with new leaven
I AM STILL because HE IS REAL!

He's the beginning and the end
No need to pretend
Forget what you heard

God has the last word
Lover of my soul
Dressed me in confidence
So, now I stand bold
Never again to be sold

He's the one who suffered and
The one who died
For all the foolish things I did
But then tried to hide

He's my doctor, lawyer, father,
Mother, sister, brother
Like no other, my whole life He covers
He is my beauty that will never age
He is why I keep coming to the stage
I'm America's Next Top Model of victory
If you want to know if He can really save you, just look at me

To recite a cute little poem, I did not come
Like Neo in the Matrix, I am the one;
To make a difference in this world that's major
Using the gifts given to me by the Savior
There is nothing beyond my reach
I came from The One who created when He'd speak

Here's a revelation for me and for you
We're made from the same fabric as Him
So, the same things we can do
For each one of you God has a resurrection
TELL THE DEVIL IT'S OVER!
Let God take control and give you new direction

Duania Hall

Duania Hall is a motivational speaker who aims to help others live their best life after trauma. She shares her personal experiences and life lessons with a poetic style that touches the soul. She hosted the poetry venue Speak Out Loud in Inglewood, CA. and facilitates empowerment writing workshops throughout Riverside County. Duania was featured in LA. Focus "Through the Storm," sharing her testimony as a survivor of domestic violence. She currently uses her platform to educate communities about domestic violence and motivate people to get involved in prevention. Duania's goal is to be a catalyst of healing for women and teen girls suffering from domestic violence.

You can learn more about Duania at facebook.com/duania.hall or contact her at dkhallfirst@gmail.com.

Overcoming the Abuses of Business Culture
By Deidre Helberg

Do not be overcome by evil, but overcome evil with good.
Romans 12:21 NIV

The light shines in darkness and yet the darkness has not overcome it.
John 1:5 ESV

I am an overcomer. I am a fourth-generation business owner, not a fourth-generation business. One must understand that there is a difference. I was blessed to see Black business owners and professionals throughout my life. Growing up, I was taught to have your own. My grandfather and my parents owned their own businesses.

As a New Yorker, I have dealt with bigotry and sexism most of my life. It was not unusual for a man to say to me, "You're a woman. How are you in the electrical field?" In my mind, I recognized his ignorance about women in the field. However, one man continued to say, "I wouldn't loan you any money." Ironically, we were attending a forum that was supposed to help minority and women-owned businesses. The struggle to overcome the abuse of business culture is constant—but I will see justice.

Internalized racism. Self-hatred. Sexism. This intersectionality attacks a Black woman's emotional, physical, social, economic, and professional being. This abuse affects us in every way. When your womanhood is attacked and you attempt to defend yourself, you are labeled as an angry Black woman. Your self-esteem is continuously challenged. However, your moral compass must remain intact.

For example, I had a scheduled meeting with a larger electrical distributor. When I walked in, the contractor saw me and remarked to his colleague, "You didn't tell me how cute she is. You're not a real business." I was curious to understand what he meant by saying my company was not a 'real business.' As the conversation ensued, his business proposal did not meet our bottom line. I smiled, said thank you, and left. I learned that every proposition is not a good proposition. Do not compromise your values; remember that the truth always prevails.

I will never forget walking into a big meeting at one of the trade organization offices. As soon as I walk through the door, one of the men turned around and told me how he preferred his coffee. In that moment, as I looked around the conference room, I noticed that everyone had a tent card with first initial and last name next to their chair. I pulled out my chair and said, "Good morning, Dee Helberg." I found myself sitting right next to the man who was telling me how to make his coffee.

The man sitting across from Mr. Coffee was big in stature, looking like a lineman from a football team. He burst out laughing and said, "If you didn't know what a redneck is, you just met one." As he continued to laugh, I sat there really trying to hold my face completely expressionless. I thought, *Dear God, get me through this because I really want to slap this man.*

I was angry because I am not the help. As a Black woman, I have the talent, skills, and ability to lead a company with dignity and professionalism. I will not compromise my standards. The words of Alice Walker resound clearly in my ear: "The most common way people give up their power is by thinking they don't have any."

At one conference I attended, a diversity officer—a White male working for Lehman Brothers—informed me that I couldn't possibly know what I was doing in the electrical industry. I thought, *This must be some sort of joke.* I was furious. I walked away, swallowing hard because of the way he spoke to me. Another gentleman who overheard what was said invited me to his booth. He gave me a sympathy order of approximately $20,000. A couple of years later, the same diversity officer was out of work when Lehman Brothers went out of business. Helberg Electrical Supply is still standing!

I am an overcomer. Although my light shines, I am often still treated as invisible when in the room. I believe women of all races should work to elevate one another; however, I know it's not always the case. During an MWBE (Minority Women Business Enterprise) and MBE (Minority Business Enterprise) Conference in Long Island, I had almost secured a major contract. Once the woman in charge discovered a Black woman behind the name Helberg, I heard the words: "Oh, I didn't know you were a minority." My last name often opens doors for me. At the same time, I will never forget how she made being a minority business owner sound like something dirty. She did move forward with the bid, just not with my company. Sisters of all races, we must love and support one another because when you win, we win; when you lose, we lose. Let's stop tearing one another down and realize we *all* have value.

I am an overcomer. I had the audacity to launch my own business and I was marginalized because of it. My journey almost came to an end when I suffered an ischemic stroke in January 2020. In prior years, I had heart disease, and yet I am still standing. I am grateful to God that He canceled my expiration date, and I could see His grace. The intersectionality of internalized racism, self-hatred, and sexism continues to attack my emotional, physical, social, and professional being as a Black woman. This abuse affects us in every way. When your womanhood is attacked, you attempt to defend yourself, and you are labeled an angry Black woman. However, I overcame this when I realized that abusers are insecure, and it is they who have the problem. Breaking the silence is the only way to move forward and soar.

Yes, my self-esteem has continuously been challenged. Yet I know who I am. I know the investment my parents and grandparents made. I know the legacy they left behind. I know my spiritual inheritance and the power I possess. I can still see the black diamond with its luminous glow.

The pandemic has brought everything to light; we are at a place where the good, the bad, and the ugly are roaring. This world and our nation is suffering. The pandemic has exposed what we as Black women have experienced—emotional, mental, psychological, and cultural challenges during an economic crisis. It is painful and killing us softly. Sisters, we can overcome character assassination. Intersectionality is a word that every Black woman should be familiar with, for we all have a story. I decided to tell my story about overcoming the various forms of abuse within the business culture. Often women may not recognize or even acknowledge that they are being abused. Or that they are perpetuating the abuse. However, *my* name is Deidre Helberg. I am an overcomer. And I am still standing.

"We may encounter many defeats, but we must not be defeated."
Maya Angelou

Deidre Helberg

Deidre Helberg, a New York native, is the Pres. & CEO of Helberg Electrical Supply. She is married to her husband for over 33 years. She is the mother of three children and grandmother of four grandchildren. Mrs. Helberg is active in civic organizations as well as African American Women organizations.

She currently serves as the President of the U.S. Coalition of Black Woman Businesses. As Deidre continues to run the business, she is motivated to support other business owners and influence her community on an economic level. With her years of experience and hard work, she is determined to fulfill her goal of changing their lives for the better.

www.hesep.com
Sales@hesep.com

The Silent SCREAMS of an Army Wife
By Dr. Tracie Hines Lashley

"A wife of noble character who can find... She is worth far more than rubies."
Proverbs 31:10

A fluttering heart with screams of excitement, chills throughout my body, a racing mind, and so many other emotions overtaking my being as I scream "YES" to his question... "Will you marry me?" Little did I know... I would soon be married to the military, not the man that I fell so madly in love with.

"A man who finds a wife finds a treasure, and he receives favor from the LORD."
Proverbs 18:22

Love at FIRST SIGHT. Literally
Pregnant and already a single parent of a precious little boy, I traveled 10 hours to take a scary journey to a new life. So many emotions were inside as I traveled this long and lonely road from Florida, where I was born and raised for 23 years, to North Carolina. I had so many expectations, but I knew one thing... I WILL NOT marry a military man. I did not want that life and swore that it would never be.

After arriving at my destination, I was tired and worn out from the drive. Traveling with a toddler and pregnant is not fun. I walked into my mother's apartment and just quietly sat for a while. I did not know what my life would be like in this foreign place. What kind of job will I find? Who is going to hire me five months pregnant? I was so scared. Guess what? I was about to be even more terrified as my mother, Valinda Russell (at the time), that she was taking me down to the welfare office. WHAT!!! Who me??? I will NOT.

I was so humiliated to need government assistance after leaving home where I always had two jobs and doing rather good for myself. Why did I leave? I wanted to start a new life. Thirteen days into my new life, I went to Fort Bragg with my cousin. I could not find her but will eventually run into this guy with the most gorgeous smile that I have ever seen. YEP!!! You guested it… It was my future husband, Rodney Lashley. I just knew that he would be mine.

"The more time you invest in a marriage, the more valuable it becomes."
Amy Grant

Wearing the Pants and Dress

We married after 3½ years of dating. We now were a blended family of five. Rodney was sent off for months at a time, which would leave me to take care of the home. It is not easy juggling life on your own when you have gotten used to someone being there to help. I was forced to raise three of our children alone, which included taking them to their practices, games, recitals, and more. Homelife was not a place where I wanted to see chaos. I married to be with my best friend forever.

The struggle of being broke in the military and missing my husband from a distance was not an easy task. We struggled so much over the years that I am surprised that we made it ten years. The shame of asking for food from the dining facility (DFAC) at night was so heart wrenching. How can we be broke when he is in the military? Easy!!! The military salary forces your spouse to have a high paying job, in most cases. I was not born to live an average or "just getting by" lifestyle. I wanted my children to have the ability to have choices and afford to be in sports, band, and other activities. There were so many times when we would worry about having enough money for uniforms or instruments.

"Sometimes your heart needs more to accept what your mind already knows."
Unknown

The Devil Wears Boots

We were so in love, but I knew that something would happen to our love due to military life. There were many times when he would come home, and we had to get to know each other again. How can that happen? When you separate for a year a time, some emotions and changes happen to people. We are not the same people. We must continue to grow and form new habits. Well…. As he continued to deploy, we would soon grow apart regardless of how much we tried to stay whole. You never know what goes through a person's mind when put in dangerous situations like a roller coaster ride.

The many deployments (11 in 20 years to be exact) were weighing on our marriage. Male and female soldiers were leaving their families for months to a year at a time. This will cause wandering eyes or mixed emotions and feelings when you are unsure if you will return home walking off the plane or being carried off in a body bag. No one knows the thoughts that wander in a soldier's mind when away from their family. This type of atmosphere also weighs on the spouses back home. The unknown is heartbreaking. Are we to be apart, and you do you, and I do me? Are we to just sit and worry about what the other is doing? What do you do?

"You never know how strong you are until being strong is the only choice you have."
Unknown

Stolen Memories

Post-traumatic stress disorder (PTSD) is nothing to take lightly. This disorder makes it difficult for people to recover after the experience or witness to a terrifying event. My dear husband was in war zones so often that he changed. This was no longer the man that I married. This was a man who continued to step in and out of my life frequently. I would have to be introduced to him each time, and vice versa. I was lost and did not know how to deal with the changes. I feel that he was trying to learn to cope, as well. When he would leave, the children would also be different. Our environment would change, as well. Each time he returned home; I would have made drastic changes to our home. I was not aware that I had changed the environment that he remembered, which may have caused confusion or distance. This is something that the military does not prepare you for.

"What counts in making a happy marriage is not so much how compatible you are but how you deal with incompatibility."
Leo Tolstoy

Disappearance of You

After ten years of an emotional rollercoaster ride, we would divorce and stay distant for about two years... Satan won... I lost my best friend, my homie, my soulmate, my everything... How can I go on after this? What am I going to do? This is something that was NOT supposed to happen. His family did not believe in divorce, but my family did. I was used to seeing family members get divorced, including my own parents. The only people who I saw remain married were my grandparents, Raymond and Martha Russell. They stayed together for over 60 years until the passing of my grandfather.

"Being deeply loved by someone gives you strength, while loving someone deeply gives you courage."
Lao Tzu

God's Promise

Two years of finding Tracie again would soon lead me to a place where I would seek God for answers. I had the typical questions that many of us have. "Why me, God?" "What did I do wrong?" "Why do you hate me?" The military took my husband away from me. I was slowly dying for so many years that I could not see God in the mix.

There was a lot of pushing and pulling on us over the years after our divorce. There was even a moment when I started feeling like I was in the song "The Boy is Mine" that Brandy and Monica released in the 90s. We played with the idea of mending things and pulling our family back together, but Satan was still holding on tight. But my faith was stronger than the tight grip that Satan thought he had on us.

God will take you through to have a testimony for others. I am now allowing God to turn my MESS into a MESSage. After six years apart and a roller coaster ride, God reunited us, and we remarried. You see, the devil was using the military to break what God set in place. When you listen to God and walk in the path… that allows him to be your compass, the possibilities are ENDLESS!

You do not marry the person you can live with…
…you marry the person you cannot live without

LESSONS LEARNED:

- Never turn your back away from God
- God is always there
- God will turn your MESS into a MESSage
- Trust the process and keep moving forward
- Never allow your current situation to define you
- FAITH over fear will ALWAYS WIN!

Dr. Tracie Hines Lashley

Dr. Tracie Hines Lashley is a child of God, wife, mother, and grandmother. As a working mother and college student for ten years, she had to find a sense of balance while juggling her children's activities and not losing herself in the process. She now helps working mothers and women in leadership positions harmonize their life while creating dynamic and productive teams at home and work. Her purpose in life is to transform the lives of others by inspiring, equipping, and growing. Her mission in life is to provide leaders with the tools required to ignite an intentional growth mindset that will drive behavior to achieve actionable results of personal value. Her vision is to see women reach their full potential, remove obstacles and knowledge gaps, and LEAD their life vs. just LIVING their life.

Dr. Lashley can be reached at info@drtracielashley.com. You may also visit http://drtracielashley.info, http://theligsllc.info, or https://bossdupleadherz.org.

Within the Ropes... In God's Hands!
By Michele Irby Johnson

"For it was not an enemy that reproached me; then I could have borne it: neither was it he that hated me that did magnify himself against me; then I would have hid myself from him: But it was thou, a man mine equal, my guide, and mine acquaintance. We took sweet counsel together and walked unto the house of God in company."
Psalm 55:12-14

There is nothing like being in the fight of your life, especially when you played some part in it. My story began when I was struggling with being single after a divorce and trying to live my life as God intended. This was one of those life experiences that I did not see coming entirely. I was in a season in my life when I had no dating prospects years after my divorce... There was no one in particular interested in me as a single mother with a young son. I would often find myself asking God, "Why doesn't anyone love me?" Is there anyone who wanted me? Looking back, I realize those were very destructive questions. They were questions that would ultimately land me within the ropes of a fight that I could not possibly win on my own.

Have you ever asked God for something, and you ended up regretting it? Yes, I found myself in a proverbial boxing ring fighting for my life rather than in the safety of a healthy, loving relationship that I desired. I allowed myself to be captivated by the lure of what I thought was a love that would take care of me... a love that would see me as a person with feelings, with a heart, with dreams and aspirations...a love that would do me no harm. Admittedly, I lowered my standards to become someone's significant other. I allowed myself to get into the ring with someone so that I could be part of "a couple." I wanted to be like others that I saw… those who appeared to be happy and in love. I wanted to belong to someone, and they belong to me. I wanted to have the security of a tangible relationship (not the one that I often fantasized about) that secured me, and that was sanctioned by God.

I thought I understood what it meant to follow the commands of God, but I found myself compromising my faith to be in a romantic relationship. Desperation took a front seat, and discernment took the seat at the rear of an extremely long passenger train. I pushed it as far away as possible, thinking that accessing it would be more difficult if I kept it at a considerable distance. To my chagrin, I needed discernment more than I cared to admit.

So, here I was, lonely and longing for love, and when this six-foot four-inch gentleman steps into my office, lighting my life up with his winning smile. To me, he appeared to be just what I was looking for… He appeared to be what I needed at the time. He was charming, funny, and was extremely attentive from our first meeting. He asked if he could borrow some of my cassette tapes (this tells you how long ago this was). I was so drawn in by his charm that I gave him the cassettes and immediately accepted his invitation to dinner. Who would have thought that I would be exchanging cassette tapes for my faith, commitment to God, and ultimately my life?

He and I quickly became inseparable. In retrospect, it all happened too quickly. I was so enamored by his presence, his attention, his closeness, his concern for my safety, and his wanting to know my whereabouts at all times that I ignorantly overlooked the beginning stages of power and control. What started as a whirlwind love affair quickly turned into something undesired. Before long, I began to experience the subtle coercive control actions of intimidation, jealousy, demeaning words, and jeering stares, which he justified as love. The mental, emotional, and verbal abuse then followed, but I excused his behavior as something that would eventually pass, and we would be just fine.

The first instance of physical abuse occurred when I went to his apartment and told him that I did not think that this relationship would work out. I realized that I did not like the controlling aspect of his love. He responded by shoving me to the ground and kicking me. In terror, I pleaded with him, apologizing, and saying that I didn't mean it. Instead of him hearing my plea, he dragged me to the window, pushed the top half of my body through the window (he lived on the 11th floor), as he placed the knife to my throat. He said if he could not have me, no one could have me. I screamed and thank God; there was a knock on the door. He released me to answer the door. In his brief absence, I was able to get myself together. I grabbed my purse and ran.

I returned to work, and confidentially shared the incident with my supervisor. I was so visibly shaken that she told me to go home and relax. After a week apart from him and a trip out of town, I was constantly being barraged by his calls. I finally answered and agreed to let him talk it out. He was relentlessly apologetic. He cried. He begged. He told me how much he loved me and that he would never do anything like that again. During a church revival, I clearly heard God tell me to leave him alone, but out of fear of being alone, desperation, and dare I say, stupidity, I ignored what I heard and eventually married this man.

Guess what? He lied, and I fell for it! Throughout the marriage, I experienced every form of abuse at his hands, including repeated spousal rape, choking, nearly having my hands broken, beatings while I prayed, isolation, blame, threats to my life, my co-workers, and my livelihood. I felt like I was in the middle of a boxing ring with my arms tied, and my wellbeing suppressed under his power. I fought within myself every day. I was going out of my mind. Whenever he wanted to "show me," he would send the boys outside, and I was left alone exposed to his violent frenzy. With each physical assault that I experienced, God entered the room and caused something to distract this man from carrying out the unthinkable. I told God that if He saved me from this mess that I caused; I would NEVER be so desperate to choose my flesh over my faith again.

It took me being in this situation to relate to what I've only heard about or saw in the movies. I endured an abusive relationship thinking I could change him… Thinking he needed me… Thinking I deserved the abuse or believing that the children needed us to stay together… Thinking no one understands and asking what people will say if they found out? I was in a caustic prison daily. When I moved, he moved. Where I went, he went. I was losing myself. I was living in a tornadic reality with no apparent means of escape. With every encounter at this man's hands, God's hands were protecting me from impending death or irreparable damage. One day God's loving hands provided the unexpected opportunity for me to escape, and I never looked back.

While living within the ropes, I did not readily find the strength to leave. I made excuses for the abuse, and I tried to convince myself that he didn't mean it until I saw my life pass before my eyes regularly. Beyond the abuse itself, there came a time that I had to see my own value and the truth of God's love for me. I realized that my life is worth more than any love outside of the love God has for me. Exchanging my self-worth for the notion of being in love was no longer an option. Twenty-two years ago, I chose ME over counterfeit love. I chose God's plan and purpose over my desires and dreams and have found my value and my voice and now understand the consequences of every choice that I make.

Many women in abusive relationships are not so fortunate to escape their abuser. Since I escaped from my abusive marriage, it has been my life's passion to help women to thrive after they survive their domestic violence ordeal. My lived experience postured me to become a transformational coach to walk women from a place of violence to a place of victory. Helping women to see their lives outside of the violence has its own reward. Although I participated in the mess, God's hands led me out of a place of pain and into a place of empowerment, strength, courage, resilience, and tenacity.

Michele Irby Johnson

Michele Irby Johnson is a disabled veteran, survivor of domestic violence, wife, mother, speaker, trainer, coach, Talk Show Host, Pastor, and educator. She is a published author of two literary works, Love's TKO: A Testimony of Abuse, Victory and Healing and Grace for Your Journey: Sermons of Survival in the Wilderness. She believes that every experience has been providential in shaping her into the woman she is today. She EMPOWERS individuals and organizations to reach their full potential and purpose, TRANSFORMING them from a posture of complacency to being able to ENVISION their tomorrow TODAY! To experience Michele's work and ministry, visit www.iam-mij.com, www.livingbygraceministries.org, and www.kingdomcbi.org. Watch her on YouTube at Life Matters with Michele TV Official and at Grace Point TV Official. She is intentional in all that she does to leave God's footprint in the spirit of those she encounters… Her living is not in vain!

Black Roses In Concrete
By Davina Jackson

The smell of chlorine and night air surrounded me as I held the hotel key tightly in my hand. Tears rolled down like rivers of salt that had no ending place; see if a spear could be thrown at God's eyes, she would aim for them. How did you get here? How did you get here? God cannot love me as they say, for if that was true, why was I struck by a car at eight years old? Why was I raped and almost shot at 15 and left to figure it out alone? Why didn't my parents see me? Wait, why was I given kids with challenges, and why did babies die in my belly, and why did he not love me after 23 years of marriage? And why does dating make you feel less?

The rivers flowed so heavy from my eyes I could no longer see the waves in the pool. God, why am I here? My heart cannot take this pain anymore. Jump! Jump! Sink to the bottom. They deserve a better mother than you. You are homeless and broke, three special needs kids in a hotel room, and you have nothing now. No designer bags, shoes, cars, baby pictures. Gone. My eyes roll deeper back, and more tears flow as I peek in the door, and they sit watching television. See, they laugh as I realize I only have on the panties I ran out of the house with. I hate you! I hate you! See, at this point, I hated God for the pain, the dirt he continued to throw on me. They say if you believe His Word, you have joy. Well, that was a lie, or so I thought it was. See, I had had rough times in life and always prevailed. Never realizing that wasn't me, it was God letting me grow just a little before he would change my soil. As a young girl, I prayed Jesus make me like you and Oprah...

what was I asking? And why did he hate me, you know Jesus the one who covers?

As I pulled my tears together and counted my five dollars, I began to walk the parking lot. Watching people carry clothes, and the smell of failure filled the air, I knew I had to produce dinner out of the five dollars. So off to McDonald's, I went crying and pleading with God about this pain I couldn't bear. I remember standing in line thinking, "Damn, how do we eat in the morning" As I strolled slowly back to the room, hoping for no questions of "mom, where are we going or are we gonna be ok"? See, I had no answer, just hope. Hope that despite my anger that maybe God did love me, and this was a bad dream.

Well, you guessed it, no dream, I woke up with a pain in my neck as I slept in the desk chair, so my kids had the beds and saw it was real; I was homeless and almost broke. So, I humbled myself and called a friend for money, she blessed me, and we could eat; I washed clothes in the tub until more friends hit my CashApp. Little did they know they were all I had, and if they stopped, so would my world, well so I thought. I found some coins, and more donations allowed the days to turn into weeks of walking to wash small items bought in the dollar store and cheap meals of free food and McChicken's. These days seemed endless as the nights filled my eyes with salty tears burning of the uncertainty of what life would bring us. See, the storm came again as my son vomited from stress and fear, and his brother also. Children with autism need stability and balance. All while not knowing my daughter feared me not coming back from a walk. I began to feel weary and yet strong. I realized that Jesus did love me because we were surviving, and I did not jump, and when I ran, I returned to them.

As those hotel days turned into weeks, I began to people watch, walk more, and began my relationship with the only man I realized never quit on me. Yes, the one I even hated (Jesus). As we began our nightly chats at the pool or as I strolled the hotel parking lot. I began to hear him say he was growing me, and I needed all the dirt he had thrown in life—each time, I needed replanting to grow bigger and stronger. Sometimes, we do not realize when the pot is getting too small, and we need replanting. I remember a sweet smell filled the air, and thoughts of my grandmother's words filled the sky. Why do you worry, child?

For I know the plans I have for you," declares the Lord, "plans to prosper you and not to harm you, plans to give you hope and a future."
JEREMIAH 29:11 NIV

Then I began to feel my hands sweat; my throat began to close, I shook uncontrollably and began to cry and feel the presence of wanting to vomit as I began to see visions of my rape, hearing his words and remembering the smell of alcohol and the gun beside me. I hear the gunshots through the window, walking the street in the dark alone at ten because your parents forgot you, the anger of pushing out dead babies and hearing your spouse say "your worthless and no one would want you' as he chokes you and slams you on the floor. And now you see the cracks in the concrete, and they look like all the broken pieces of your life. I began to shout and cry and say, "why am I stuck in the purgatory of life?" God save my children and all who were like me. This poured from my lips. Not knowing I was a rose growing in concrete. See that next wonderful morning when the money ran out, I dressed and prepared to walk across the stage and get my nursing certificate as valedictorian with no idea what was next or where we would sleep. Yet money magically showed up from my birth father and heavenly Father.

It was time to leave the hotel and pain, so I found a little place and decided to sleep on the floor. But God sent all the people and things I needed. As I stood in front of an amazing group of women giving a graduation speech on greatness, I never saw mine. The days passed, I worked hard at shock trauma; until that moment, the world went from fast to slow motion. I felt the matrix; I fell straight down and broke my foot. God, you must hate me, uttered softly from my lips as tears rolled down my caramel checks. A few weeks later, surgery and screws, yup no work. As I laid quietly on the sofa, I began to ask, what do you need from me? Why am I filled with so much sadness? At that moment, I felt peace. He said, gain clarity of your heart; I have given great stamina and oil. Did you think you were alone? As I blew my nose and wiped the ever-flowing tears from my pink eyes, I remembered, through every moment, I thought I was defeated, even though the pain I was still standing. I stood through fear, through uncertainty, moments of shame and toxicity, spiritual brokenness, spiritual brokenness, moments of ugliness. See, Christians have all these moments, and we are believers. But we all must grow and be formed to be more spiritual.

Se we do not control life, God does. He never said it would be easy. See, I said I wanted to be like Jesus. So, I needed to be outcasted, made fun of, beaten, laughed upon, and even shamed Because I was no better than Him. Yet my Heavenly Father protected me and showed me why He made me. Parts of me had to die so I could be reborn. In my rebirth, I saw I was standing as a beautiful rose. At that moment, We (Jesus and I) formed Optimism Designs. But more importantly, I was formed to stand through anything.

*Trust in the Lord with all your heart, and lean not on your own understanding. (*PROVERBS 3:5)

*In all your ways acknowledge Him, and He shall direct thy paths (*PROVERBS 3:5)

*How great is the love the Father has lavished on us, that we should be called children of God! (*1 JOHN 3:1)

Know that whatever storms or rocky places you may find yourself, lean on your Heavenly Father, and trust in Him. Through it all, I am still standing.

Funny it seems, but by keeping its dreams, it learned to breathe fresh air. Long live the rose that grew from concrete when no one else ever cared.

Davina Jackson

Davina Jackson is a mother of three amazing children with Different Abilities (Disabilities). She is the "peel your onion "lady and award-winning Autism Coach, Rising Motivational Speaker, and Amazon Best Selling Author, and Minister. Teaching families not only to peel through their layers to become transformed holistically but to implement goals and understand special needs. Davina developed Optimism Designs LLC to give women, men, and people of different abilities a voice and the tools to succeed. She continues to show that all lives matter and that our success depends on our self-awareness and growth. Some families and friends call her "The Spiritual Gangsta" Davina Jackson finds creative and insightful, fun ways to bring scripture to the lives of many by apply everyday events to God's words. Bringing awareness and spiritual love to all she encounters.

https:// www.optimismdesigns.com/
optimismdesigns@gmail.com
https://www.facebook.com/Davina Jackson/
https://instgram.com/events_optimism/
COMING SOON: BUTTERFLY TRIMMERS AND MEN CRY IN THE DARK....

Destined For Purpose
By Yolanda D. James

Today, January 7, 2012, marked the foundation of my journey. On October 19, 2012, I turned 50, which is half of your life journey. For as long as I can remember, it was the last of the struggles in my life. I often look back on my life, asking why? Why did I have to take this route in life? Why did I not listen to someone who saw my future so clear who wanted to protect me from all hurt, harm, and danger? My daddy loved me so much and wanted so much more for me, but not enough to stay and watch his little girl grow up or watch his son become a man. My dad left my brother and me when I was five years old; my brother was three. This is where the problem began. There was no unity in the household. I did not have a male figure to show me how to be a lady, let alone a successful woman. There were times when my mom was so sad and lonely because she had to raise her children without the man she once thought was her soul mate: the man she trusted to take care of her forever. You see, he did not know his dad either; he could not teach or love because he was not loved himself. So, the cycle began.

During the summer of 1974, my mother and aunt decided to go to a bank teller school. That meant my brother and I had to stay at my aunt's house in the evenings. One night my aunt's husband decided to get drunk and touched me. Everything my brother and cousins did, I got beaten for it. He would beat me repeatedly with my pants down. He kept beating me because I could not move my bowels. He would take his thumb and repeatedly insert it in my rectum. What pain and agony! I got beaten for everything that the boys did, and he said I better not tell my mother.

I said I would not. He hit me and said, tell her. When I said that, I would tell. He beat me again. This went on for hours. I keep looking at the door, crying for my mother to come and ring the bell. I made many attempts to get out, but there were too many chains on the door. I hated him with all my heart and soul. I cried so much that night until it made me sick. Eventually, he fell asleep, and finally, my mother and aunt arrived. It seemed like they were gone for years. Well, my mother did not have to put my coat on. I ran past them when the door opened. It was not until I got downstairs that I heard my mother call my name. On our way home, I explained to my mother what had happened. She was furious and afraid that he had molested me. We did not live far from my aunt. When we reached home, my mom called the police, but my uncle had made his way to our house with a bottle of rubbing alcohol and a white towel sitting on a porch. The police came and took him away. In the meanwhile, we headed back to check on my aunt. She had been gagged, tied up, and put in the closet. He was a sick person.

Life Begins

Freshman year was not a good year for me. Jeremiah 1:5 had already taken place in my life. How many times do we say, I wish I knew what I know today, but just realize that God would not get the Glory if everything were perfect in our lives. We must have these experiences in life to tell our stories for someone else to be saved and delivered. Then it happened, the book of Job 2:16. However, I did not know the Lord; this life was very new to me. But God's hand was on me, as stated in the book of Ezra 7:28. Everything from this place and time would allow me to walk in my destiny and purpose. The enemy in the flesh came to destroy God's purpose for me but little did we both know that God's hand was upon me. For years I had dated guys who always depended on me to finance their lifestyle. I thought buying them would put me in a good place with them to never leave me. But since my father left me at a young age, I had no example of what it meant to be treated like a lady. I dealt with disappointment and embarrassment from people who had warned me. God had a plan for me, and this was my journey. Because my father mistreated my mother, the seed was sown in the earth. The Bible says in Galatians 6:7-8, Be not deceived: God is not mocked for whatever a man soweth that shall he also reap. I was reaping the seed from my father's decision.

Turning Point

Years went by, and I finally got married to a nightmare. My Pastor had pulled me to the side one Sunday after service and told me not to marry him. Did I listen? No! I married him anyway, never knew how to be a wife, or what marriage was about. All I know that it should good, God's hand was still on me, and even though the way I was taking was a long journey, it was all in the plan. Proverbs 3:5-6 would take residence in my life. Psalm 46:1 says God is our refuge and strength a very present help she shall not be moved; Go help her and that right early. My story's moral is - I came from a dysfunctional home setting, which allowed me to be used by men and marry before the Lord had placed me with my mate. I birthed children with a person who also was not raised by a man, only a single parent.

There was never any structure, so my daughter became the product of my mistakes - running away, lesbians, drug dealers, prostitution, and so much more. My husband became a crack cocaine addict for 28 years. I was stressed, confused, angry, and suicidal. I went from job to job, trying to ensure that all bills were paid, and we had a roof over our head. But my husband felt the need to steal and sell everything that I had worked hard for, even the children's school clothes. I struggled with health issues to almost death from bleeding from fibroids. Not only this, but my youngest daughter decided that she would get pregnant at the age of 15, which meant I had to be responsible for her, the baby, and everyone else. I was so angry at life and what it offered me, but I had to take responsibility for what I chose to allow in my life. But trouble never seemed to end. I was ordained as a minister during the time of my daughter's pregnancy. But why, Lord, how did this come about? I was embarrassed and ashamed of what was going on in my life. A drug-addicted husband, the oldest daughter was into homosexuality; the middle daughter was running with drug kingpins, but I never gave up or stopped praying.

New Addition

January 8, 2004, my granddaughter was born dead, but the James 5:16 EFFECTUAL prayer of the righteous man availed much. I had taken care of my daughter and the baby on an $8.00 per hour job. God had put people in my path to help me along the way. During this time, my husband had been arrested and sentenced to 20 years in prison, and I stood by his side each for the whole time. He did ten years, came home, and went back in six months. I knew this was my key to a divorce. Enough had been enough.

After five years of taking care of my granddaughter, I gave her back to her mom. I took back my life and all the things that God had promised me. I was able to get a divorce and move on with my life. I lost 180 pounds along with the 250 of a man that had me bound and weighed down. This was when the spirit of the Lord birthed in me Anointed Women of a Greater Call International Outreach Ministry. My story is just bits and pieces of my life journey. My book detailing the harsh realities of what I went through can be purchased on Amazon.com. I tell my story to so many women who are afraid of change in their lives. Be Free and Live Life.

Yolanda D. James

Yolanda James is a native of Newark, New Jersey. She is a Hello ordained minister and a Licensed Pastor, Social worker, Inspirational Life Coach, Humanitarian. I received my calling at the age of 21. I accepted the assignment for my divine destiny when the Lord birthed in my spirit, Anointed Women of a Greater Call International Outreach ministry, which is a ministry for the whole body of Christ. I am the CEO /Founder of Choose She 'T' Shirts Designs BY YO. And the Founder of People with Zeal LLC. I am the author of I survived the Journey. I have traveled to different parts of the world for coaching, mentoring, and outreach ministry. I have set on the Board of Directors for Families First of Richmond Virginia, Advocate for Reinvested Communities, Seedling Foundation, Austin Partners in Education, Austin Black Caucus Association. She loves traveling, horseback riding, bowling, shopping. I am currently working on a mentor program for women and young adults in Jamaica; I am also a part of Mentor Her Ghana.

My contact information is womenonfrontline@gmail.com. You can also purchase my book on amazon.com.

Rejection, My Reality Adjusting Superpower
By Raechelle "Rae" Johnson

"Poured my life w/out measure into a little treasure box I thought I found..." These are the lyrics from one of my favorite songs, CeCe Winan's Alabaster Box.

I remember like it was yesterday. I watched the Chief of Staff walk from her office walk down the hall to the Pastor's Office. I heard her talking to the Executive Assistant of the Pastor as their voices disappeared into his office. Then I watched one by one as the Director of Operations, the Director of Finance, and the Director of Human Resource came from the Lower Administrative Suite to the Upper Administrative Suite down to the Pastor's Office. It did not strike me as odd until the Pastor contacted me and, "Raechelle, can you come to my office, please?."

At this point in my life, I had experienced so much rejection. Maybe not more than anyone else but to me, it felt like rejection had found me, moved in, and decorated. At this point in my life, I felt completely alone. I was estranged from my family, not seeing eye to eye, not sure where or always how to fit in; my relationship had crashed and burned, and I was left to raise our son totally and competently alone, feeling inadequate and insecure as a mother and woman; doing it on my own with a high school diploma I had already been subjected to classism, sexism, and racism. So, when I was asked to interview for a position supporting the ministry that I attributed to saving my life at a time when the part of my life that had value was being a mother, I was ecstatic. Up to this point, I was finding small treasure boxes to pour myself into and being disappointed time after time losing what I had left. It was getting harder and harder to stand. See, I believed there was more to me than I was projecting that anyone could see, but life keeps giving blows, and I could not catch my breath, let alone a break. But now, I would be serving to the fullest and do so in ministry.

I moved from working in an administrative capacity for the Lower Level Administrative Suite to the Assistant Office Manager in the Upper Administrative Suite to the dual role of Office Manager and the Administrative Assistant to the Pastor. I served on multiple ministries and even led a few. There were challenges along the way. I was surprised by the nature of some of the clergy I worked alongside, but people are people; we are all flawed. My feelings were hurt often, but I kept in mind that I represented Christ, the Ministry, the Church/Pastor, and I, and my feelings were not even secondary.

I walked back to the Pastor's office, and everyone was seated in his office that never looked so small and uninviting with everyone crowed around and seated. "Have a seat Raechelle." Something told me to stand, so I responded by respectfully declining. He suggested that we go to his study and all getting comfortable. When we moved to the study, everyone sat, and I noticed that no one sat near me. Pastor ask was it better, and I brought to his attention that no one in this larger setting wanted to sit near me. I spent most of that meeting noticing how it took longer than it ever had, how I did not see it coming this time, but how familiar this scene was. I was out of place.

I had played by the rules laid out, I kept my head down, I did what was asked, and I did my very best, but somehow I still wound up on the outskirt of the group. As they each took their turn explaining what it was, they wanted to be done differently or better; it was all superficial.

The bottom line was I had out voiced my position and who I had become innately made them uncomfortable, and they wanted me to become more compliant and manageable.

Then it happened years later. After accepting my role in the background while presenting work for the foreground and handing it off to the persons selected to lead, to run with it, it clicked. I was not good enough. And that caused my existential crisis. I worked in the lane created for me without question, acceptant of the terms as they were laid out when the Executive Director came to me and shared with me the shift. He informed me that the Receptionist would be replacing me as the Administrative Assistant to the Pastor, assuming the title of Executive to the Bishop [as he recently been elevated to the new office] I would remain Office Manager. She would take over my office, and I would move an office in the Lower Level. I could not process the information as it was being relayed to me. I just kept going over in my head conversations about the part-time receptionist I wanted to promote to a full-time administrative assistant that was rejected because she did not have the skillset, but she now had the skill set to assume a position higher than mine and assume my office.

This was not a rejection; this was his older, much meaner, and stronger brother. Have you ever been hit so hard you do not know you have been hit? Is this what punch-drunk feels like? He called my name, and I looked at him. He asked if I had any questions, and I shook my head no. Questions that I did not understand. Some time went by, and I began to process the absurdity of what was happening and had questions, so I requested a sit down with then Executive Assistant to the Pastor soon to be Executive Director.

On the day of the meeting, I walked into the Pastor's Study to see the Director Operations, the Executive Director, and the Pastor. I had so many questions; I felt so betrayed, but then I remembered the scene from years before, and I surrendered. I did not have any fight left. I was asked what my questions were. And out of the 25 questions I had prepared, I only wanted three answered. "When will the change take place," "What are we telling people," and "Who is responsible for what?"

However, the entire time the question that was circling in my mind was, "God, what is wrong with me? Why do I continue to find myself here?

Every time I find a place of comfort [my little treasure box], the place where I can serve, and rest, I am not just shown the exit; I am pushed out, isolated, rejected. I couldn't find comfort at home, the man I was in love with was in love with others; I had wrapped my life and the life of my son up in this ministry; all I had personally and professionally was here. My identity was here. They say falling isn't falling if it doesn't hurt when you hit the ground; well, I hit so hard I wasn't sure I could get up. For the next 30 days, I remember walking around dazed. A barely spoken whisper breaks my trance in the hall during the workweek and in the pews during service. I wasn't eating or sleeping, and my hair started to fall out. I couldn't even hear from heaven. It wasn't until one day, my son came to me and mentioned that his mentor pulled him to the side to console him. To tell him not to let the talk around the build bother him. Although they were replacing his mother with a prettier model, I was still an attractive woman. Is that what I did wrong? I wasn't small enough, cute enough. I couldn't begin to process this for myself, let alone try to do damage control for my son. Was that the source of the whispers? Comparison is the devil, but self-doubt is a true runner up. An Evangelist/Organizational Leader I respect once said where there is friction, there is no oil. So, if the anointing has left, you need to follow suit. I put in my letter of resignation in March of 2006.

I left the ministry in 2013. It took me seven complete years to realize that I was called to a platform of greater. I do not have the luxury to become complacent on assignment in the marketplace or ministry. It is all about position and timing. It is imperative for me to be in the right place at the right time. As an Innovation Strategist, I help organizations and individuals address the consumer of tomorrow's wants and needs.

My superpower is foresight, innovation, and growth. And if I get comfortable, I will be made to be uncomfortable so that I will move on at a steady pace. I am Raechelle "Rae" Johnson, the Solution Architect, and I am still standing.

Raechelle "Rae" Johnson

Raechelle Rae Johnson, the Solution Architect, is an International Motivational Speaker, Coach, Business Strategist, TV Host, Author, and Owner of Kreative Ink LLC. She provides real-world solutions for early-stage small business to large lead generating organizations and individuals in innovative and strategic learning and development support. With the goal of improving knowledge and skills to improve capacity for solving problems, managing future change, and meeting strategic and tactical goals, she has designed, implemented, and lead the organizational transformation from diagnoses, action planning, and implementation to evaluation and continuous process training program(s) for 900+ of the Fortune 1000 organizations, all four major sports leagues, all six branches of the U.S. Armed Forces, and the three branches of the federal government. With me, you create your definition of success.

To connect for opportunities, feel free to contact me
Website Https://www.Kreativeinkllc.com
Https://www.Facebook.com/KreativInkllc/
Https://www.Instagram.com/Kreative.ink.llc/
Https://www.KreativeInkAppt.as.me.

The Things I Know For Sure
By Paula Johnson Hutchinson

The year 2020 has been one that many of us will never forget. It has been filled with an unknown pandemic that has changed the course of history. Each month has been wrought with updated information, canceled vacations, virtual learning, and lots of online meetings. All over the world, there is a level of uncertainty that has plagued the year. We have all had to endure living in a time where whatever is planned is subject to change.

Through it all, some things have a sense of familiarity to them. It seems like we have been here before. The sounds, the tears, the frustration of postponing sparks familiar emotions. It could be a feeling of anxiety. It could be the feeling that today's "no" will be infinite. We close our eyes, take deep breaths, wipe tears, delete emails, scroll through social media, and have this feeling that where we are now, it exactly what our timeline will look like in the upcoming years. Are we focused on problems or solutions? Are we using our faith or attempting to operate in our human flesh? Are we using our own gifts or measuring our success based on what someone posted online? Are we focusing on our God-given promise, or are we trying to Google God?

The Bible states that faith is the assurance of things hoped for (Hebrews 11:11). This means that no matter what is going on around us, and sometimes that is pure hell, our faith is our hope. It is our lifeline. If we all think about our life experiences, some things simply cannot be explained in the natural. That negative bank account that now continues to grow us... faith. That extra sleep that replaced the sleepless nights...faith. The degree that we thought was impossible...faith. The new love that made us forget the bad one...faith. The sickness that we have overcome...faith. The will to move on, after all, has been lost...faith—the power to move on from 2020...FAITH.

When the history books are written about this time, and there will be many written, there are some things that we all will know for sure. How will we know? Because of our faith, which is the "assurance," we will know that we can move forward. We will know that we are survivors; we will know that we can adapt. We will know that our goals are adjustable. We will know that we can remain connected. We will know that our joy can return. The benefits of our faith are all around us. Even when we feel that we can go another step, take another, call, take more bad news, take another report, take another closure...our faith carries us to our next. Our faith will be solidified because we will be the evidence that we did not fold. We did not break, even when we had to bend. We will learn that we can stretch beyond our wildest imagination. This time in history will be our testimony. Sharing our testimony is how we provide instructions to the next generation and the non-believer. Our testimonies of this time will not be filled with exaggerated bragging. Nobody living and surviving this time in history needs to add anything extra. This time is evident that we can conquer even amid the unknown and adversity. Those testimonies will inspire those who cannot see their way. They will know that success is a possibility.

Hebrews 10:24-25 states that we should consider how to motivate one another, not neglect to meet together, and encourage one another. So, I will share the things that I now know as of today for sure. I know that that connections matter. Even in the darkest of time, I have found a reason to smile by the connections I chose to nurture. We cheer each other on. We meet online and do drive-by events so that we can see each other's faces. I know that protecting your peace can save a lot of heaviness. We are not meant to carry the weight of everyone. We can become so top-heavy with everyone else's business that we neglect our purpose and selves. We cannot pour from an empty cup, and attempt to try will not pay high dividends. Instead, it can make us hate what we love. We can become so heavenly bound, attempting to save everyone else, that we are no earthly good. Whatever our time on this planet is precious for sure. Just because you slid out of bed should be enough to shout right there. Your ability to take in a living breath is the oxygen of opportunity, and you're very being. I know that I can adjust. Deadlines can be moved, and delays of pandemics or the inability to travel should not necessarily mean the end of dreams. I know that I can adapt. We all have learned that we still need to pay our bills, save money, and take care of our kids. We are doing that with what we knew before and have learned during this period. I know that goodbyes are necessary. Slowing down allowed me the time to clean up my relationships and discontinue life-stealing vibrations from others that were blowing their negative residue in my direction. I know that our stories matter. Sharing with my children, connections, mother, and spouse have made me so proud to be in the space I am in. I know that past life experiences prepared me for such a time as this. What would have broken me down in the past, I learned to take those same brick of defeat and build. I know for sure that time is precious. It waits for not one soul. It moves whether we want it to or not, and when time is up, there is nothing that can make us go back. Like time, we must move forward to the days ahead.

The biggest lesson I know for sure that this too shall pass. Everything we are going through is for a purpose, even if it is not always immediate as to the "why." What breaks us down often makes us available to hear the voice of God. He has equipped us with the Holy Spirit, and when we are obedient to our inner selves, we often emerge better than before. I know that we all are resilient and powerful in our own way. And I know for sure that we did not come this far to be left out here to nothing. There is something greater ahead; this, I know for sure.

Paula Johnson Hutchinson

Paula Johnson Hutchinson is a serial entrepreneur that began in the beauty industry. Since then, her platform has grown from beyond the chair to include speaking, podcasting, consulting, and training. She is also the creator and founder of The Stiletto Talks which is a safe space for women of color that provides encouragement, motivation, and education.

Coming Out of the Closet
By Lois Larkins

Paul wrote in Romans 12:12, "Rejoice in our confident hope. Be patient in trouble, and keep on praying." When asked, "from what am I still standing?" my answer is the loss of family members; through death, betrayal, and wrath. My story began on December 12, 2019.

That day I lost two grandsons as the result of a murder-suicide incident. Despondent and grieving like I never grieved before, I received a notice for jury duty. My cousin, whom I will call Ebolina, called my doctor, hoping he would prescribe something to help me rest and provide me with a medical excuse from jury duty. He said, "'No,' and it is my duty to serve my country." I'll not tell you my reply to him, other than I reminded him that wholly apart from my emotional state, he prescribed physical therapy for back pain due to spinal stenosis, sends me to a neurologist, a rheumatologist and that he should read the medical reports provided to him. During this time, Ebolina and I were very close. We were close because she knew that her mother, my first cousin, and I loved each other as sisters. I considered Ebolina not as a second cousin but as a niece, and she always said to me, "I got your back, Aunt Lois Ann, and I'll always be here for you." She most likely said this to make me feel better because she saw that my daughter had not been involved in my medical care.

On the morning of December 31, 2019, Ebolina physically threatened me. She grabbed and threw my handbag on the street, breaking the cell phones that were in it. I had to pay over $1200 to replace the phones.

You see, she became jealous that my daughter, whom I will call Kimalina, volunteered to accompany me to my doctor's appointment that afternoon. Ebolina reminded me that she had accompanied me to many medical appointments though my daughter had not made herself available time after time. Ebolina did have a point, but I was hoping that Kimalina was finally getting it and that she would be there for me. Several months later, I found out via a group text while dealing with family drama after a much-loved cousin passed away that Ebolina told Kimalina that I had lost my mind and attacked her on December 31. After that, for whatever reason, they became the best of friends. Now, as a health-challenged "baby boomer," I would truly have lost my mind if, first of all, I fought someone I loved and treated like a daughter, helped her in her times of need, and who is a tall and healthy "baby bust." Suffice to say, Ebolina's betrayal severed our relationship.

At the age of sixteen years old, my daughter began to disrespect me on many occasions. I always swept those incidents under the rug just to keep the peace, but I never imagined she would get physical with me. However, on March 7, 2020, she snapped and physically attacked me, throwing me to the floor and beating me with her fists. What a traumatic experience. For over twenty-three years, I lived in Florida, and in 2011 my daughter asked me to move back to Maryland and live with her. So, I sold my properties and moved back to Maryland. In 2017 she asked me to leave, and I did but left some furniture stored in her house, or I should say the furniture she decided not to send to me. At that time, I was having serious health challenges. I was having partial seizures due to a lupus flare-up and didn't know it.

Feeling too ill to relocate to Florida, I became fearful, and I married a friend. He had always asked me to marry him so that he could take care of me. Just what I needed. He is a good provider; however, he has been angry with me for the past two years because I made his doctor aware of his erratic driving habits. He was diagnosed with dementia and narcolepsy, along with other medical issues, and his driver's license was revoked. He blames me for the loss of his driver's license.

Back to Kimalina. I didn't know when she asked me to leave, but later found out she was preparing to have a former boyfriend back in her life and move in with her. Unfortunately, she had a volatile relationship with this man in the late 1980s, and their relationship is still volatile. I let him know I disapproved of their relationship; nonetheless, he respected me for being upfront and often asked me to pray for him. I did and prayed he would be able to improve himself. I am still disheartened when I look at the text Kimalina sent me a few months back saying that he had attacked her in her own home. I am sad for both Kimalina and Ebolina. This sadness was only intensified when Kimalina physically attacked me in March when I sought to retrieve some of my furniture from her house.

While enduring the demonic attacks and COVID-19 shut down, I moved to the basement of my home, which, of course, makes me feel isolated and lonely. I have done this both because my spouse goes out frequently and because of my autoimmune issues. Oh yes, the pandemic stopped my fellowship with church members and going to gospel concerts, which were outlets for me. Not having my daughter and cousin check on me nor offer to get food for me digs at my soul. Strife is not good for any of us. Every day, I thank God for my church family and a couple of friends who check on me from time to time. God is a provider, and when I go into my prayer closet that He provides for me and shut the door, I pray to my Father in private, and He, who sees everything, rewards me. He blesses my soul and guides me in making the following P.R.A.Y.E.R. I am to:

Put on all of His armor so that I will be able to stand firm against all strategies of the devil; believe He will give me patience for when my faith is tested, my faith has a chance to grow.

Race in this life, and it does not mean that I will be the fastest runner and always win, nor will I be the strongest and always win the battle, but know that the rise of any weapon will not be able to turn against me.

Abundantly live life for this is His purpose for me and know that He can keep me from falling and will bring me with great joy into His glorious presence without a single fault. Hallelujah!

Yield myself to my Lord and take His yoke upon me and let Him teach me for He is humble and gentle at heart, and allows me to find rest for my soul; and know that He, Jesus Christ, is the same yesterday, today, and forever.

Enter His gates with thanksgiving, go into His courts with praise, give thanks to Him, praise His name, be earnest in prayer, confess my sins to and pray for others, and if I do, I will have great power while producing wonderful results.

Rejoice with a glorious, inexpressible joy because I love Him even though I have never seen Him, but I trust Him, and I shall humble myself before Him and resist the devil, who will flee from me.

When coming out of the closet – my prayer closet - I no longer feel beat up or beat down or messed up or pressed down; I am just too blessed to be stressed. I hope you are encouraged by the scriptures from which I have spoken. Allow me to share my favorite quote with you. English evangelist, Leonard Ravenhill, wrote in 1959:

"No man is greater than his prayer life. The pastor who is not praying is playing; the people who are not praying are straying. The pulpit can be a shop window to display one's talents; the prayer closet allows no showing off."

When was the last time you were in your prayer closet? Go in now and pray to your heavenly Father with the knowledge that prayer changes things, and the first thing it changes is you. I thank God for the revelations He has given me. I have grieved, felt betrayed and disappointed, then sad, but now I am glad. I count it all joy that I have met my various trials.

When you are going through troubling times, know that you are not alone – a little lonely perhaps – but not alone. Be sure to read and meditate on God's word, wait, ask for wisdom, and you will come through on the other side standing tall.

Lois Larkins

Ms. Lois Larkins is an ordained minister and says that you may address her as elder, evangelist, or minister but not reverend. Lois heard the Lord's call in 1994 to preach the gospel and has persistently been active as a servant for the Lord since.

From 1973 to 2010 Lois made her livelihood as a Legal Secretary working in Washington DC and Miami FL; Word Processing Supervisor; Software Trainer; Technical Writer; Microsoft Computer System Engineer (MCSE); and owned her own business which provided network and information technology support.

Lois has attained numerous Certifications relating to both computers and ministry; a couple of degrees in church ministry and is most proud of the degree she has received from God; Praising Him Daily (PHD). Currently, she is working on her first book to be published in January 2022.

Email: Lois@imognetworks.com, Twitter: @Lslarkins, FB/LinkedIn: Lois Larkins, and IG: Loislarkins111.

From SCRIBBLE... TO SCRIBE!
By Chanda London

A man's gift maketh room for him, and bringeth him before great men.
Proverbs 18:16 (KJV)

I'm still standing after experiencing a life-changing Spiritual New Birth forty years ago in 1980 at 18 years old. Three months later, I stepped out on faith, impromptu, and preached my first sermon. Later received ecclesiastical training under great leadership, which proved invaluable, laying a strong foundation for the next transition that would further hone me towards a prolific destiny.

I began Inspiring Nations in 1988 after being greatly impacted at a Conference in Wilmington, Delaware, where the Honorable Bishop Norman L. Wagner of Youngstown, Ohio, ministered, "A Call to be Water Walkers." It was while inflight home to California that God said to me, "WHEN YOU GET HOME, DON'T GO BACK TO YOUR CORPORATE JOB, GO TO THE CHURCH AND WHATEVER YOUR HANDS FIND TO DO, DO IT!"

The next day, I went to the church and volunteered. Three days later, I prayed for God to grant me favor that if it is His Will, let them offer me a paid position by the end of the week. The end of the week came, and I hadn't received an offer; so, I said goodbye to the staff and thought to myself that I will return to my corporate job on Monday. Notwithstanding, as I walked towards my car, one of the staff persons ran into the parking lot, saying to me, "WAIT A MINUTE, DON'T LEAVE! THE BISHOP SAID TO "TELL CHANDA, I NEED HER TOMORROW TO TAKE MINUTES AT THE BISHOP'S BOARD MEETING!" Not being a secretary and NEVER having taken minutes before, I was reluctant; however, the person who relayed the message persuaded me to do so, saying she would pray for me.

Unbeknownst to me, years later, the same person told me what had actually happened: I HAD DIVINELY LEFT 'A PIECE OF PAPER' ON THE DESK AT THE CHURCH OFFICE THE DAY I VOLUNTEERED. (It was a phone message for one of the office staff that I had written in shorthand and forgot to throw it away after transcribing it!)

SHORTHAND: a system of rapid handwriting, employing simple strokes and other symbols to represent words or phrases; often referred to as 'SCRIBBLE.'

She went on to say, "THE BISHOP PICKED UP THE 'PIECE OF PAPER' WITH THE SO-CALLED 'SCRIBBLE' ON IT" AND ASKED HER (in his strong, stern robust voice!): "WHOSE IS THIS?!" Her reply was, "O THAT'S CHANDA… SCRIBBLING AGAIN!"

With haste, she took the paper from him, balled it up, and threw it in the trash. (What she didn't know at the time, was that he knew shorthand as well!)

The next day, while sitting in the meeting with renowned clergymen and women from around the globe, sweating nervously, I began to SCRIBBLE with the pen of a ready writer. My shorthand speed at the time was 110 words per minute, so for me, they weren't speaking fast enough! While they discussed agenda items, I began to teach myself how to write in shorthand new words that were common to them but foreign to me, such as Ecclesiastical ('ih-klee-zee-as-ti-kuh l'). All of a sudden, one of the pastors from San Jose, California, interrupted the protocol of "Roberts Rules of Order" that The Honorable Presiding Bishop Wayne S. Davis strictly abided by and asked with a loud voice, "CAN SISTER LONDON BE OUR SECRETARY FOR THE WEEK?!" I lifted my head and wondered what he was talking about; the Presiding Bishop said, "If the Pastor from San Jose would like to ask a question, the Chair will entertain!" The countryfied pastor repeated his demand slowly and said, "CAN... SISTER LONDON... BE OUR 'SEK-RI-TER-EE' FOR DA WEEK?!"

Immediately another Pastor from San Diego, California, "SECONDED" his request! The Presiding Bishop hit his gavel and declared, "IT IS SO MOVED!!!" And just like that... I went from SCRIBBLE... TO SCRIBE!!!

SCRIBE: One involved in copying manuscripts and other texts and Secretarial and Administrative duties, including the taking of Shorthand dictation and the keeping of business and historical records within the Episcopal Office.

After taking a leap of faith, God's Divine Plan for my life manifested before my eyes into what would now become my destiny From SCRIBBLE... TO SCRIBE!!! At the end of the week, I received what I had asked God for, the organization had 'hired' me as their part-time SCRIBE. Two weeks later, the Presiding Bishop's Executive Secretary resigned and recommended I take over her position. There again, just like that... I went From SCRIBBLE... TO SCRIBE!!!

In May 1993, one month after enduring the unexpected demise of the Presiding Bishop W. S. Davis; I found myself Still Standing by the Grace of God. Afterward, I began receiving several phone calls from a colleague (WHO HAPPENED TO BE THE SAME PERSON WHO HAD ASCRIBED ME AS "...SCRIBBLING AGAIN!") asking if I would consider relocating to Youngstown, Ohio to work in ministry with Bishop Wagner. On each call, she shared with me some of the work they were doing, concluding with the statement: "...IF THERE WAS ONLY A CHANDA!"

Knowing my ministry assignment was over in Inglewood, California, I was open to a possible change. Therefore, I traveled to Youngstown, Ohio, only to discover there were no beaches nor two-story malls! (Being a native of Los Angeles, California, this was major!) Therefore, I gladly got on the plane after my visit and returned home.

The next day, while driving on a major freeway on my way to work at the church office in Inglewood, I heard The Voice of God come through the sunroof of my car saying, "YOU ARE WHAT I PROMISED HIM." I asked The Lord, Who? He said, "BISHOP WAGNER." GOD told me, "BISHOP WAGNER PRAYED FOR SOMETHING AND YOU (CHANDA) ARE THE PRODUCT (THE ANSWER TO HIS PRAYER)!"

Three months later, in August 1993, I traveled to Port of Spain, Trinidad, to assist as I had annually for the past five years in the OMNI Conference's facilitation. This is where time met destiny. Bishop Wagner was in attendance and extended me an invitation to attend his Annual Pentecost In Perspective Leadership Conference in Youngstown, Ohio, in September. While attending the Youngstown conference, he asked me to attend several impromptu meetings and take shorthand dictation, which led to an invitation to join his Executive Staff as Executive Assistant in International Affairs. Once again... I went From SCRIBBLE... TO SCRIBE!!!

It was on the heel of relocating to Ohio, in May 1993, that I became a Christian entrepreneur and established Stones Of Help International Ministries, Inc. (SOHIM INC.™) to provide platforms for Global Ministry Development.

In November 1993, I had the esteemed privilege of traveling throughout Europe on Bishop Wagner's International Ministry Team

Inspiring Nations, developing the administrative structure within the Continental European Council, which included Germany, England, Italy, France, Belgium, and Ireland. I was then appointed to serve as an International Executive Liaison to the Europe Council, and just like that… once again, I went From SCRIBBLE… TO SCRIBE!!!

On many occasions, I recall Bishop Wagner speaking well of me, ascribing me as:

Called to be an Evangelist

Clothed with the Mantle of an Apostle in her gift of Administration

Endowed with a Pastoral Anointing

A Gifted and Inspirational Teacher

One who Heralds her Prophetic Voice to the Nations

After enduring nearly 20 years of full-time ministry in Youngstown, Ohio, I experienced for the second time, another loss: the sudden and unexpected demise of my Presiding Bishop N. L. Wagner. Nevertheless, I'm Still Standing as I continue to remain committed to serve as International Executive Liaison and SCRIBE to the European Council of Nations.

As a SCRIBE in The Lords Church, I've been afforded many great and incredible opportunities Inspiring Nations to incorporate administrative protocols within the local church office and by adding administrative structure to a variety of church ministries. Such notoriety gained me the honor of being requested by several Global Organizational Pastors to train their Church Secretaries, Administrative Staff, and Pastoral and Ministerial Staff throughout the USA, Trinidad, and Europe.

In 2009, I became a self-published author and SCRIBED a book entitled, "The JACOB Generation".

I took another leap of faith in 2011 and returned to Corporate America, working for an airline. In 2013, I relocated back home to Los Angeles, California, and started a second career as an International Flight Attendant with the world's largest, global airline while remaining committed to the SOHIM Inc.™

As we dawned this new decade, 2020, I began to "…SCRIBBLE AGAIN!" As SCRIBE, I launched the "CHANDA LONDON GLOBAL MINISTRIES" at the SOHIM Global Office in Cerritos, California, USA, with endeavors to continue Inspiring Nations conducting weekly Virtual Inspirational Teaching Sessions known as "SOHIM Ministry Apprenticeships."

And the LORD answered me, and said, Write the vision, and make [it] plain upon tables, that he may run that readeth it.
Habakkuk 2:2 (KJV)

Chanda London

Chanda is an anointed woman of God from Los Angeles, California. For 40 years, she demonstrated Multi-Dimensional Excellence in Ministry as well as diverse, adaptive Professional expertise. She parlays these attributes into effective ministry, distinguishing her as a qualified International Evangelist, Inspirational Teacher, International Executive Administrator, International Travel Consultant, Global Flight Attendant and Self-Publishing Author of a unique magazine-style Readers Digest: "SOHIM GLOBAL" and two books, "The JACOB Generation" and Volume 1, Anthology Book Series with 8 Co-Authors entitled, "BORROWED VESSELS: Women Pouring Out."

Currently ministers to the Nations from her Global Office in California; Virtual Inspirational Teaching Sessions weekly known as "SOHIM GLOBAL Ministry Apprenticeships."

More details relating to the Chanda London Global Ministries can be found on our Website: www.chandalondon.com. You can also connect via E-mail: chandalondon@mail.com.

Problems to Proverbs: My Journey to Womanhood

By Ayana Maia, The Capacity Coach

There I was, alone in my kitchen, tears flowing down my face, sitting on the floor with a knife at my throat. I was ready to end it.

Life had become so mentally overwhelming, and I was emotionally depleted that I gave up on life; I gave being a mom, a wife, a daughter, a sister, and a friend. I couldn't live up to the titles. I gave up on being a woman of God because, after all, what kind of woman was I that he would want? I felt like I was drowning, and I couldn't catch my breath, and every time I tried, the chances of survival seemed slim to none.

Imagine drowning to death, then you come back to life only to die by drowning again, and this cycle repeated itself over and over again. This is how suffocating and defeating my life felt, and I was at the end of me.

I was failing as a mother, outnumbered one to four with no direction, overwhelmed, and relationally disconnected. I hadn't taken the time to heal from the trauma of my first marriage fully, and I was still struggling with childhood wounds like rejection and abandonment. Both only compounded the challenges I had as a wife in my current marriage. I lost my way, lost my identity; I could no longer see my value, and felt worthless. I lost touch with my friends and family and felt very alone. My walk with Christ was so new that I was still learning what it meant to walk with him. I was in over my head, and there I sat, empty, ready to die.

I thought about my loved ones one last time; with the knife to my throat, I closed my eyes and took a deep breath. As I exhaled and prepared to slice my throat, I heard God whisper, "ask for help." I immediately opened my eyes, loosened the grip on my knife, and tears started to well up. Hearing his voice shifted something in me. I wasn't alone. He was with me. Ironically, in obedience, I picked up my phone, navigated to my church Facebook group for wives, and posted that I'm ready to end it. I do not want to live anymore, and I'm not sure what to do. I'm not sure why this group or these women, but God's plan was in motion. Within minutes I had women flooding my phone with texts, calls, and responses to my post – all with a resounding message of, this is NOT what God wants for you. You are SO LOVED, and WE love you. I read their pleas and affirmations with tears rolling down my face. My heart was filled with love and support. I dropped the knife and wept. I knew God was right there with me.

I believed that only good things came from God; that he would never bring harm to me. I now understand that God can use that same thing for your good when something is meant for evil – self-inflicted or by others. God had plans for my suicide attempt. He knew what was going to happen, and his provisions would help me heal; I just needed to have faith and trust the process.

I believed God didn't want a woman like me, broken and flawed. My womanhood looked nothing like that of a Proverbs 31 woman. I wanted to end my life because I was failing in my titles, i.e., a mom, but it was more than that; it was about who I was as a woman and how my character dictated how I showed up in each of those titles. I didn't know the characteristics of being a godly woman, and he was about to birth in me his divine purpose for women and womanhood.

With a renewed commitment to live, over the next couple of years, he revealed to me women of the Bible who had tremendous courage, strength, wisdom, and faith despite their trials. He showed me how women pushed through their challenges, and he used Bible studies to draw me near to him. That's when he empowered me with the term Ezer Kenegdo.

Ezer Kenegdo is the Hebrew term used in the Old Testament for a helpmeet. Upon further study, I learned that Ezer, in Hebrew, means to rescue or save, to be a strength or power. God is an Ezer to us, and he instilled the same quality in women. Do you know that it is entirely impossible to help anyone without some strength, power, or ability? Women are strength for the weak, power for the powerless; we are sanctuaries for the weary, and encouragers for the discouraged. Women are warriors. We go to battle every day for our family, our livelihood, and ourselves.

Kenegdo means one who is the same as others (man) and who surrounds, protects, aids, helps, and supports, having strength or power that corresponds to man. We do not have the same role man is, but we sure were designed to be an equal source of strength that compliments man. This blew my mind! You mean to tell me, simply being a woman is my superpower? It's how I help! Sis, did you catch that? As a woman, you were fashioned to be a powerhouse on purpose! My appreciation for being a woman and the authority that came with it increased. Now, I'm not saying this is a permission slip to be reckless and exert your power maliciously, but I want you to understand just how powerful your womanhood is. It is a strength that can move a nation and save lives. When I was in that space of wanting end my life, it was a group of women who rallied around me. Do you hear me? WOMEN! A community of women saved my life!

After discovering this, I decided to become the woman I was destined to be. It was not as some subservient wife, or an emotionally absent mother, or a faithless woman. I was called to be a woman of God and a warrior in womanhood. A warrior is someone who is engaged and experienced in warfare, someone who shows great vigor, courage, and boldness. As warriors, we are to intercede in prayer over and for our family, be operational leaders/COO of our households, and active voices in our relationships.

Transforming into a warrior comes in stages and will be a lifelong journey. I fight every day to resist the dark and become light. I feel like the chains are breaking off, and I can free my kids from generational curses. I want the same for you!

Here are three tangible ways for you to jumpstart your journey, break from bondage, and become a warrior in womanhood:

1. Ezer Kenegdo: Start here! Study this. Work to understand the fullness of this term and how it applies to you as a woman. I studied this until God solidified the meaning of it my heart.

2. The Word: Go into your Word! I suggest doing specialized 30-day scripture studies (available on my website). God helped me understand the Word from his perspective, taught me how to get in his presence, and how to pray. It strengthened my relationship with Christ, and my self-worth increased.

3. Community – Build Your Tribe: I sought out like-minded women, in groups and individually, that I could lean on, pray with, laugh with, and cry with. They carried me through very challenging moments. They are my warriors in womanhood. My community now includes a therapist, an elder, and an accountability partner, three of my best investments.

I hope that in sharing my story, you too will make a new decision to keep going, to rise up, and take ownership of who you are. That you become inspired and encouraged to show up and be the woman God has called you to be. It's hard…I know. Sis, if you need help, I'm here! Whether it's coaching or community, you do not have to do this alone.

Let's connect! I would love to hear from you, support you, and be a warrior in womanhood!

No more sitting by the wayside, waiting for life to happen. Warriors cannot walk in bondage. Break free from negative beliefs. You are a Woman of God – a Warrior in Womanhood!

Embrace your inner warrior, sis!

Imagine who she would be if she showed up.

Imagine the light she would become for the darkness of someone else.

Imagine just how divine her purpose is.

Did you just have a moment? Because I sure did! Sis, the world needs YOU to show up!

I AM A WARRIOR, and so are YOU! So, keep pushing, keep moving forward, keep standing. Someone out there needs YOUR light. It's time to show up!

I dedicate this story to the Warrior in Womanhood, to Ezer Kenegdo, to Strong Women. May we know them. May we be them. May we raise them. Amen.

Ayana Maia, The Capacity Coach

Ayana Maia is an HR professional with over ten years in the field. Specializing in employee relations and training and development, Ayana uses her DISC certification to help employees reach their full potential. As the Capacity Coach, Ayana offers a business development program for entrepreneurs and small startups, along with a variety of HR-Related services. She is also passionate about women's empowerment and runs an online community for women. When not in her professional capacities, she enjoys spending time with her husband and four children.

To learn more about Ayana, book a service, or download the resources mentioned in this chapter, visit: www.thecapacitycoach.com or follow her on social media: @thecapacitycoach @ayanamaia.

Too Dark for Love
By Shelley Meche'tte

I remember being so excited. I can't remember my actual age, but I don't think I was any older than about 6. I asked my mom to do my hair. I remember getting all dressed up. He was coming to see me. He promised to be there this time... **again**. *This time* would be different. *This time*, he'd keep his promise. *This time*, he would show.

Upstairs in the one-bedroom apartment that I shared with my mom was a huge, long window that sat behind an equally long curtain in the homey living room made just for us. The window went from just below the ceiling all the way to the floor and stretched across the wall. Of course, as a young child... it could've seemed *extra*-large because I was so small.

After my mom dressed me in what I believe was a yellow dress, with little ruffles at the bottom (making me feel so special)... I waited... on the floor... behind the long curtain... in the huge window. And I waited... and waited some more. Eventually, my eyes begin to tire, and my heart began to break. I continued to wait, though... ultimately being rocked to sleep by the teardrops flowing down my cheeks.

I can still remember the soft touch of my mother cradling me in her arms as she picked me up off the floor and took me to our room. She laid me on the bed, gently undressed me, and placed me in my pajamas. She took my pretty ponytails down and covered me for the night.

Once again… his promise had been no good. He had left me waiting in the window, excited to see him dash up the stairs with that slight grin that I could barely remember then and remember even less now.

He was my father. Little did I know it then, but his toxic habit of unreliability would harmfully impact how I viewed myself, men, and relationships for a long time. At the time, I didn't understand that the effects of repeatedly being lied to, feelings of abandonment, and being pushed aside would follow me and subconsciously become one of the driving forces for both successes and challenges in my life.

Growing up, I always knew that I was unattractive. The world told me so. There was nothing *special* about me. Nothing that made me "pretty." I wasn't light-skinned. Not even a nice cocoa brown. Nope. I was dark. I didn't have pretty hair. No curls, no waves. No sleek ponytail with just water. Oh, no. My *simple ponytails*… took **work**! I didn't have light eyes. Just your regular 'ole brown. Nothing special about that. And I wasn't bi-racial. So, therefore, I was not attractive.

Other than my mom… no one consistently poured life into me. And while I don't necessarily remember her *telling* me that I was "pretty" throughout childhood, I knew she loved me with her entire heart. I was a mama's girl, and we both knew it. My mother made me believe that I could do **anything**. There was no limit to who I was or what I could become. Anything I put my mind to, coupled with a solid plan, was achievable for me… simply because… my mother said so!! I needed that confidence. I needed someone to help me see past the "dark girl" in the mirror and the low ceiling that society kept offering me.

As I grew, trying to continuously convince myself that I was *enough* became a struggle. I was constantly battling myself. Yes, I was this confident girl who believed that she could accomplish anything. But I was also the ugly girl who understood that she would never get "the guy." At least, not the guy she wanted. I would never have "options," like other girls… because of my skin-tone. I'd have to learn to simply accept (to a degree) whoever wanted to be with me, whether I really liked him or not. I knew I shouldn't have to settle. I knew I was a great catch. But I also knew that no one really wanted to "catch" me… a dark-skinned girl.

I knew this because more than one guy had told me this. The circumstances surrounding the memory are a bit foggy, but the words and feelings that came with those words aren't. Over the phone, a young man I was interested in made things very clear when he said, *I would never date a dark-skinned girl. I don't care how pretty she is. I only go-with light-skinned girls.* Whoa! I was shattered. Just like that day in the window, I wasn't worthy. I wasn't *enough*. And because of my complexion, I never would be.

Then, there was the awesome day that I "courageously" told a young man at my church that I had a crush on him. I say *"courageously"* because I told him that I liked him by pretending to cough while saying the words. Afterward, I walked out of the room to finishing "coughing," just in case those feelings weren't reciprocated. Well, not only were they not reciprocated, but he proceeded to explain that we could never be together because if we ever married, we couldn't have children. Since he was already of a darker complexion, having children with me meant… "our kids would be too dark."

I'm not sure what was more devastating. The words themselves or the fact that the devastation was coming from *his* mouth. He would later marry a light-complexioned woman.

I would later find myself in the fight of my life… as a verbally and emotionally abused woman!

I met *David* while working in the mall. David was brown, medium height, and cute. There was even a shyness to him that I found to be quite adorable. We seemed to vibe in those short moments of meeting, so instead of waiting for him to ask for my number, I elected to offer it to him. He gladly obliged... smiled and walked out the door.

A cute guy had *caught* the "dark girl." YES!

I have often been asked, what happened? What were the signs? How did things go from sweet bliss to emotional battery? The truth of the matter is... I just don't know. I never knew what verbal or emotional abuse looked like. I always equated abuse with physical harm. So when "Shelley" slowly became replaced with "b****," "ho," "slut," "stupid," "fat," and then some, I was already in too deep. While I started out standing up for myself and "putting him in his place," what I didn't realize is that my soul was being butchered, my esteem was being bludgeoned, and my identity was being erased.

I became a shell of a person; pretending to be in a fairy-tale relationship...all the while, being manipulated into thinking that me nor my feelings mattered, being controlled, monitored and even borderline stalked... to the point of him sitting in front of my house at insane hours, waiting to "catch me" cheating. Never happened.

Daily berating became the norm. I was yelled at, called names, publicly embarrassed, made fun of, and more. Then came the pushing, shoving, and slamming into walls. He even went so far as to throw dirt at me one night, as I stood there with tears filling my eyes.

That night, however, was the beginning of the end. Even with previous hurts and self-esteem woes, I knew that I deserved more than a man viciously throwing dirt at me while spewing words of hatred. Ironically though, David left *me*... for a light-skinned girl with long curly hair, who was (in his words) *"much prettier"* than me.

190

Although David was gone, his *presence* wasn't. Well into adulthood, motherhood, and even marriage, the pain of David's words and actions frequently crept back into my life... until the day that I found myself weeping in the mirror due to the residue of his abuse. I had unknowingly spent years trying to prove David's words false instead of living out God's truths. The truth being that... I **WAS** ENOUGH! Always had been. Always would be. I had been **created** with value, purpose, and in God's image. Since childhood, the enemy had been trying to snatch the seed that God had planted, hoping it would never take root.

BUT GOD!

When I began to seek God's face, speak God's words, and walk in the purpose-designed specifically for me... I began to understand my power, worth, and **every ounce** of my beauty... including my **beautiful dark skin!** I no longer granted others access to damage my being with the lies of their inferiority. I began to master... the Master's call on my life, which included empowering women to discover and master theirs!

Today I stand proud, with scars... empowered by my will to win. I'M STILL STANDING, even after being *pinned* many times. I'm not special. No "superpowers." I'm just a woman who one day decided that she would always and forever be... ENOUGH!

And guess what? YOU... are enough too!

Shelley Meche'tte

Certified Life Purpose Coach, Self-awareness Expert, and International Speaker Shelley Meche' tte is extremely passionate and dedicated to women's empowerment through strategized personal and professional development. She is the founder of the women's organization, The PowHERful Woman.

Shelley specializes in decluttering her clients' thoughts, connecting their gifts and talents to their passion, personalized Life Strategies for continual success. She positions women to live beyond their titles by helping them discover and walk in Purpose.

Some of her features include CBS, NBC, ABC, The CW, Yahoo, Bustle, Bakersfield News, Out Loud with Claudia Jordan, and more.

Shelley is the author of the books 70 Days of Happy: Life is BETTER When You Smile and PowHER Minds: Reflective Thoughts Designed for the Everyday PowHER Woman and Her Legacies.

Shelley is also an ordained Minister. She has been married since 2002 and is the mother of two amazing Legacies (daughters).

www.ShelleyMechette.com
IG: @ShelleyMechette

Still Worthy Without A Womb
By Sheryta Horne Melton

I remember it clearly. I walked into the emergency room, collapsed into a chair just a few feet away from the registration desk, and wondered, is this it? Is this the moment when I check out of here? In a waiting room, surrounded by people, yet still alone. This cannot be how my life ends, just fading to black. But that is exactly how I felt. 2015 was a force to be reckoned with. You see, after two blood transfusions, a few blackout moments, no solid diagnosis, and a very strange skin altering medicine (that ultimately served no purpose), I realized that life was literally draining from me. The scary part was that nothing was working. Anemic wasn't the word for it. I felt and watched the life drain from my body for eight months straight, which, to me, seemed like an eternity. It took my strength. It took my dignity. And ultimately, it tampered with my strength as a woman. Yet, by the grace of God, I'm here to tell you about it.

Can you imagine going from healthy, happy, and full of energy to lifeless unproductive and depressed, in just a matter of weeks? I went from traveling, running hard, and working seven days a week to barely being able to stay awake for a few hours at a time. I would go to work at 8:30 in the morning and be exhausted (and sometimes asleep) by 11:00 am. I had two children under the age of 12 to care for. I couldn't make them dinner. I used my brief burst of afternoon energy to make a food run before passing out again at 6:00 pm. It was horrible. I could barely watch a movie with them. I couldn't sit up to play a game. I couldn't even stay awake long enough to listen to them talk. Sadly, all of this stemmed from what was supposed to help and not hurt me.

In December 2014, I spoke with my doctor about the horrible pain and heavy bleeding I experienced month after month for over 20 years. It seemed to be getting worse and worse instead of better. As with many women, I was prescribed a contraceptive to supposedly "balance things out." This time it was an injection that I had never had before. The first few months were okay, and by the fourth month, my life would never be the same. It seems that the injection given to with the intent of healing would become what I consider to be the biggest hindrance to my physical and emotional health. This quickly took me down a path of declining health. I started losing pools of blood at a time. I had to change clothes multiple times in the middle of the workday. I was going through packages of feminine products a day or two at a time. I was embarrassed because I was spending 50% of my awake time hiding in the restroom. I was tired of my life being dominated by this issue. I stopped going out in public, stop traveling, and for a little while, I stopped living. Life was literally draining out of me. And there seemed not to be any viable help insight.

So here I am in this place of hopelessness. Every other week I was visiting or talking with my doctor on the phone, trying desperately to find a solution. There were days when I felt like I could deal with this situation and overcome it. Then there were days that I would wake up in pools of fluid and immediately burst into tears while scrubbing my bed for the umpteenth time and tossing out yet another set of sheets. We did the norm. I increased my iron intake and stayed on top of daily supplements. I ate iron-enriched foods. I exercised. I even ate beets! I tried everything to shock my body back to normal, and nothing worked.

My first overnight stay in the hospital resulted in my first experience with a blood transfusion and being sent home to "get better." At the time, I thought, okay, God, surely that was the pinnacle, and this is my testimony for this year. Okay, I accept that, and I'm ready for my healing now. Unfortunately, that was not the end. After a few more months of the same issue, non-stop, I was prescribed a medication that was supposed to throw me into a false menopause and stop this unruly flow. Guess what, it did not work! My body not only resisted the medication, but it also caused my skin to dry out from head to toe and created an entirely new problem to deal with. Amid that, I was back in the hospital, having my second blood transfusion. This is also the first time I hear a medical professional speak out loud that I may need a hysterectomy. And I began to sink even further.

This is the point when I truly began to question God and wonder why I would have to go through something so uncomfortable, uncontrolled, and outright unfavorable. I know we live in the 21st century, but I truly felt like an outcast from daily life. Women's health should not be a taboo topic anymore, but the truth of the matter is, not everyone wants to hear about your "issue." No matter how adversely it is affecting your life. Wear black, shower often, and keep a smile on your face. Those are our unspoken societal instructions on how to handle your problem until it just goes away. Ironically, that's how women are expected to handle many of our issues. Keep it neat and tidy and tucked away and keep smiling. No one wants to know how broken you are. No one wants to keep hearing about your problem. That is the feeling we are left with.

Imagine being in a cycle where you have constantly been losing. And the solution to the loss is... another loss. To the woman who is already on shaky ground, this is just another letdown. My mind, will, and emotions were trapped inside of a dysfunctional vessel. With no way of escape. At 37 years old, I faced what I was told was my only option, a hysterectomy. This did not sit well with me. I was already divorced, with two children, but I still had hoped to marry again and possibly have just one more child. I had a support system. But even then, I had people say things like "you already have two kids, that's enough" or "it's not that bad, you won't have to deal with monthly woes anymore." Seriously? Is that what it comes down to. I could not believe this is what the removal of my womb was being reduced to. I had a major struggle with this surgery. I know that we are talking about a scientific procedure that just meant I wouldn't have any more children. But for me, it went deeper than that. For me, it meant taking away my individual ability to produce on the earth. The idea tampered with my self-worth and my own fruitfulness. I questioned for quite a while my worth without a womb. I believe that what we see in the natural corresponds with what we see in the spirit. Did this mean I would be viewed as unproductive overall? From the outside looking in, maybe it wasn't that deep. But from the inside, trying to get out, I could not get over it.

In August 2015, the process was complete. The surgery was successful, and my eight weeks of recovery was eventful. I learned a lot about myself in that time at home, away from everything. I was forced to face myself. As a mother, minister, and leader in both the workplace and the marketplace, I had to get a grip. The big question was, am I still worthy without a womb? The answer is a resounding YES!!! I almost forgot who I was. This is the case with so many of us. We allow the bumps in our journey to diminish our value. We allow outside influences to negate our worth. Trials may try to redefine you, but your recovery speaks volumes. I want you to know you are worthy. Jeremiah 29:11 says, "For I know the thoughts that I think toward you, saith the Lord, thoughts of peace and not of evil, to give you an expected end." There is a plan in place for each of our lives. Even with moments of disappointment, we are predestined for victory. I cannot promise that adversity will not try to discourage you. But I am a living witness that we are designed to overcome. Here are four key things I want you to remember every day that you wake up. Say this with me:

1. My life has value and adds value.

2. I am fruitful and productive.

3. I know who I am.

4. I am still here.

Sheryta Horne Melton

Sheryta Horne Melton brings to the table over 20 years of leadership and business management experience. Sheryta took an interest in business and marketing throughout high school and continued studying Marketing at Morgan State University. Sheryta is also an ordained minister and is the lead instructor for ministry training at Emmanuel Empowerment Temple in Kingsland, GA. Sheryta recently completed her Bachelor of Ministry and is moving on to a Master's in Christian Business. She is the owner of Written Vision Solutions, which she founded in 2017 to serve clients through writing business plans and proposals. Written Vision has since evolved and expanded to include business development, specialized training, implementation of operational procedures. Sheryta has been successful in helping clients carve out and stay true to their vision. She enjoys assisting new entrepreneurs and is committed to coaching her clients into a position of excellence.

Visit her website at www.seewriterun.com

WOW! So, You Lost A Loved One To Cancer Too?

By Evangelist Sherrell D. Mims

"No matter what you've done for yourself or for humanity, if you can't look back on having given love and attention to your own family, what have you really accomplished?"
Lee Iacocca

Ask yourself…

How did that make you feel when your loved one was diagnosed with cancer? What stage and form was it in?

Were you sick to your stomach after getting the news?

Did you become saddened, tearful, overwhelmed, and just did not give a damn anymore?

Did you also feel like you did not want to live anymore?

Well, to answer all of these questions in one word regarding myself. YES!

As I share with you how this horrific experience impacted my mind, spirit, and soul, let me remind you, I did not ask for it, and I certainly was not prepared for it.

Read along with me as I briefly take you through the journey of my fiancé's battle with stage 4 stomach cancer from the diagnosis {June 2011} to the end of his life, {September 2013}.

Grab a box of tissue as you read my innermost thoughts and feelings on love, loss, strength, and faith.

Let me start by saying, as a caregiver, everyone deals with challenges differently in their life. What works for me may not work for you and vice versa.

I do not care what anyone says, "Cancer Sucks!" especially when it hits close to home.

The hospital journey was definitely that. It was June 2011, sunny outside with a breeze of wind blowing. So, here we are in the ER at one of the big hospitals in Fort Wayne, Indiana, in a cubicle behind the curtain. The doctor arrives and evaluates Shuggie by asking him a battery of questions. Then he ordered labs, imaging tests (abdominal ultrasound), urinalysis with culture and sensitivity to see if he was growing any bacteria in his urine, chest X-ray, and a positron tomography (PET) scan.

The PET scan is an imaging test that allows your doctor to check for disease in your body. The scan uses a special dye that has radioactive tracers to detect cancer and learn the stage. The stage describes where the cancer is, if it has spread, and if it is changing how your organs work.

As we awaited the PET results, the doctor came in with the urinalysis result, which was negative.

The doctor's main concern was the blood serum for his hemoglobin. Hemoglobin is the amount of oxygen in the blood to transport blood to the organs. Per Mayo Clinic, the normal hemoglobin range for a male is 13.5-17.5. Unfortunately, Shuggie's is 6.0!

The doctor states: "We don't know how you made it to the ER with a hemoglobin that low." We look at each other and smile. We know it was nothing but the grace of God that brought him to the ER. Praise our Almighty God!

The doctor explained that because his hemoglobin is so low, he wants to transfuse two units of packed red blood cells to get him into a safe range, at least up to 8 or 9. Shuggie agrees to the transfusion. After the two units of blood were infused by 10 or 11 pm that night, Dr. Y., the GI surgeon, came in to speak with Shuggie. He states, "I was called in on your case to do a consultation. Have you spoken with the oncologist (cancer doctor) yet?" "Yes, and I put her out of my room. She was talking all crazy, telling me what she is going to do to me. I told her to get out of here and don't come back. Send someone else." Now, the G. I. surgeon explains to Shuggie that he has the result from the abdominal ultrasound, "and it shows that you have stage 4 stomach cancer. It has not spread; it is only in the stomach area." The doctor continues, "With your permission, of course, I would like to go in and remove that area with the cancer, anastomosis (tie) the ends together, and then from there start radiation therapy as soon as possible."

Oh my God! is all I am thinking. What just happened here? Stage 4 stomach cancer. Really? Tears just started welling up in my eyes, streaming down on my face as I am sitting on the right side of the bed, holding Shuggie's hand.

Shuggie asks the doctor, "You want to do surgery on me and take out how much of my stomach?" The doctor states, "We really won't know that until we get in there, but for now, it looks like maybe half." "Doc, can you give me some time to digest this, man? This is a lot you are talking about doing. Can I get back with you later tonight or tomorrow?" "Yes, of course. But the sooner, the better," the doctor responds.

After careful consideration, Shuggie decided to have the stomach surgery performed. Moving forward to after the surgery, per Dr. Y., he comes out of the operating room to speak with the family (Shuggie's brother and myself) to let us know how successful the surgery went. He states, "the surgery was a success; however, I had to take out more of the stomach (75%) than expected because once I got in there, he had polyps and adhesions wrap around the stomach." Shuggie's brother responded, "Well, Doc, you did what you had to do. We appreciate that." I was so glad that this surgery was over.

After the surgery, Shuggie went from the hospital to rehabilitation and then home on hospice.

In my opinion, any medical technology (radiation therapy) and drugs (chemotherapy) that burns you from the inside out is not made for humans.

Now, let me fast forward you to how this affected my mind, spirit, and soul. This was a man I was engaged to be married to and spend the rest of my life's journey with, as you have read, that did not happen. We were engaged for about one year, and we never made it to the altar to seal our vows to one another.

I WAS SICK! Did you hear me? My whole being was jacked up. I hated the whole process of taking care of my loved one with cancer on hospice at home. Sure, I am a nurse. And I care for people all the time. However, that does not negate the fact that we were faced with his diagnosis unexpectedly, and I was forced to care for him, which I did not have a problem with. My problem was I felt cheated out of getting married, enjoying the rest of our lives together.

All kinds of thoughts were running through my mind.

And so, I did. I took care of God's beloved son Shuggie to the end with total help from Almighty God. Every day was not a good day; however, I looked at the positive side of things. "My help cometh from the LORD, which made heaven and earth." (Psalms 121:2, NLT).

God and I weathered the storm together. God had made it so much easier for me to deal with my day-to-day activities. Getting up in the morning was no longer a struggle for me. I knew I had to go through the storm to speak about it now in this book.

So yes, going through this tragedy over which I triumph in the end with God at the center of it all was amazing. Going through this horrific event taught me the following things:

Keep God first in your life.

Trust in the LORD with all thine heart.

Keep oneself in excellent self-care wellness.

God Over Everything!

Resources
The 4 Best Online Grief Support Groups of 2020

Find a community that helps with loss

By Amy Morin, LCSW

Fact checked by Andrea Rice Updated on June 22, 2020

Best Overall: Grieving.com

"They're one of the oldest support communities on the internet, and they support over a quarter of a million people."

MiBest Live Chat: Grief in Common

"Their site offers a live chat room that allows users to connect with others any time they would like."

Best for Young People: Hope Again

"Users might find that reading other people's stories or watching their videos help them feel less alone."

Best Social Media Group: Grief Anonymous

"Avid Facebook users might enjoy this option best, since connecting with others won't require users to join an additional website."

Five Successful Tips For Caregivers Of People With Cancer

1. Find Support : Join a cancer support group.

2. Read, Listen and Ask Questions: Go with a loved one to a doctor's appointment.

3. Stay Healthy: Your health is important too. Eat right and exercise.

4. Take Breaks: Exercise, get with a friend.

5. Stay In Touch With Friends And Community: Being with people who care about you will give you a positive attitude {texts or call}.

Reference: Cancer Caregiver Community

Evangelist Sherrell D. Mims

Evangelist Sherrell D. Mims is an author, teacher, transformational speaker, and entrepreneur. She dreams of becoming an international speaker. She received her Advanced Diploma of Biblical Studies as a Licensed Minister of the Gospel of Jesus Christ from the Destiny School of Ministry in Roseville, Michigan. She is also the founder of Beauty 4 Ashes Women Empowerment in Fort Wayne, Indiana. A registered nurse for over 20 years. Sherrell specializes in oncology, hospice, nephrology, cardiology orthopedic, trauma, neurology, and psychiatric.

Her passion in life is taking care of God's people by any means necessary. She enjoys going to church, fitness, going to the movies, listening to gospel jazz, traveling, and spending time with her daughter, Sherdell.

Website:www.mssherrellspeaks.com
Email:mssherrellspeaks@aol.com
Follow On Social Media:
- FB: mssherrellspeaks
- IG:@mssherrellspeaks

Shhh... Don't Tell Nobody
By Cynthia Mobley Howell

Mama and Daddy were two of the best Christians I had ever known. I was always led to believe that being a good Christian was supposed to keep all the bad stuff away. But if by chance bad stuff happened to come your way, Jesus would fix it all. He would wave His magic wand, and it would just disappear.

Just so you know, my family went to church EVERY Sunday at least four times, to Bible study EVERY Wednesday night, and to tarry service EVERY Friday night! I would say we had that thing about being a good Christian down pat.

Well, assuming that what I had been told was correct, can somebody please tell me how my house ended up becoming the 'Nightmare on 9th Court'? And I am NOT exaggerating.

You see, there were four of us siblings. I was the youngest and the only girl.

I knew something had gone terribly wrong when the youngest of my brothers left home after graduating from high school in the mid-seventies and made his way to New York City to pursue his dream of becoming a famous rock star but abruptly returned home a total basket case! At first, everyone thought he was just mischievous, but as time passed, we realized his actions were beyond being mischievous, and there was a HUGE problem.

I remember a particular incident that occurred that was rather bizarre. My brother visited a McDonald's restaurant and placed an order. Now, this was in the day when you paid after you received your food. So, he placed the order, and when he was served, he stood right there at the counter, ate the food, then proceeded out the door. When the staff attempted to confront him about paying, he became belligerent and combative. The police were called to the scene and were able to calm him down. After speaking with him, they gave him the proverbial slap on the wrist and released him, writing it off as a childish prank. Little did anyone know this would not be the last time my brother would have this type of episode. Yes, this was the beginning of many that would span several years.

Now, let me shift to my middle brother. He was expelled from school in the eighth grade after being accused of taking part in vandalizing a school bus. This was extremely devastating to him, and he never returned to school. We found out much later that he did not have anything to do with the vandalism and had taken the rap for his best friend. He ended up joining the Job Corp. He eventually obtained his G.E.D. and seemed to be doing fine. He left the Job Corp and returned home (this was in the late seventies), reconnected with his old girlfriend, and became engaged. Desiring a change of scenery, my brother decided to visit relatives in Miami, Florida. A few days into the visit, my aunt called my mama and said that he was behaving strangely and to please send him money to return to Panama City.

Mama sent my brother money to purchase a bus ticket, he never purchased the ticket, and no one knew what happened to the money. So, mama sent more money, but this time to my aunt. My aunt purchased the bus ticket and made sure my brother got on the bus heading back to Panama City. My family was not prepared for what we saw when my brother came through the door. The pants he was wearing were split all the way up his butt, and his luggage was virtually empty, although when he left for Miami, the suitcase was full of clothes. And just so you know, this was the brother who always looked like the guys on the cover of G.Q. magazine. In other words, he was always dressed to the nines and immaculately groomed.

The days to follow would prove to be some of the worst days of our lives. Most days, my brother would sit in one place in the house with this blank stare on his face. He would chain-smoke cigarettes all day every day. I mean, literally, smoke one cigarette right after another. We asked my aunt what happened when he was in Miami, but no one seemed to be able to shed any light on the situation. As if that was not enough, he started wearing lady's clothing. You see, mama was a maid, and the white folk she worked for would regularly give her bags of clothes, and those were the clothes he was wearing.

Remember, I told you that my brother returned from Miami with an empty suitcase. Most of his clothes were gone. So, yes, he started wearing women's clothing, and to put the icing on the cake, he decided that he would start walking me to school every day. Mind you, I was in high school, and here is this man walking with me to school every day wearing women's clothing. I cannot even begin to tell you how humiliated I was. You might wonder why I did not just tell him not to walk with me to school. Well, so that you know, that was much easier SAID than DONE. So, I just suffered in silence.

And there was my oldest brother. I remember watching him become increasingly depressed after not being able to hold down a job due to a physical illness. He had previously worked after school at a local car dealership. He had managed to buy his own car and move into his own apartment but eventually ended up moving back home because of being too sick to work and losing his job. I guess you could refer to that brother as the "quiet storm." He did not talk much, and it took a lot to upset him. But the few times that he did experience a breakdown were extremely scary! I vividly remember one frightening episode when he suffered a breakdown and was about to hit mama with a two by four. Unfortunately, I ended up taking the blow instead. As a result, I lashed out at him, which caused him to escalate, and me and everyone else who was in the house at the time had to literally run for our lives!

So, my siblings suffered from manic depression, schizophrenia, and paranoid schizophrenia.

The local Mental Health Unit and the State Hospital became a revolving door for two of them, and the third brother became a transient who just wandered from city to city. We would not see him for months, sometimes years, and then he would pop up only to leave again.

We eventually lost my oldest brother to suicide, no one has seen or heard from my middle brother for nearly two decades, and my youngest brother has been in a mental institution for the past thirty-three years.

How did I escape suffering from mental illness? I am glad you asked. It was ABSOLUTELY the grace of God! The MANY years of experiencing what I call the DRAMA and TRAUMA should have qualified me for a breakdown! Trust me when I say all the madness I witnessed living in that house could have very easily driven me over the edge! But God…

I titled my chapter "Shhh… Don't Tell Nobody" because back then and even today, mental illness is a subject that most do not like to discuss, especially in the Christian and African American communities.

It is such a shame that I "lost" all three of my siblings to the disease of mental illness. Perhaps had it been cancer, diabetes, sickle cell, or some other disease, things would have been approached differently. Unfortunately, because they had a disease that most are ashamed of and do not want to talk about, I have had to write this gut-wrenching story, and the HALF has not been told.

If corrective measures had been taken with my brothers, they would have thrived and been productive members of society.

If you or someone you love suspects symptoms of mental illness, let me suggest this:

- DO NOT be ashamed – Mental Illness is like any other disease; it just happens to affect the mind.

- DO NOT be in denial – it IS what it is. Admit there is a problem.

- SEEK professional treatment and follow the treatment plan prescribed – this one is not for the Minister. You need a psychiatrist, psychologist, therapist, or whatever discipline that is appropriate for the condition.

- FIND a strong support system – whether it be a friend, community group, etc. Make sure you surround yourself with those who can offer the love and compassion you need during your low and vulnerable moments.

I always say that if my brothers had been treated PROMPTLY and PROPERLY, things would have turned out totally different for them.

This is MY story, and I am STILL standing.

Cynthia Mobley Howell

Cynthia Mobley Howell is the CEO & Founder of CHowellMotivates, based on a CLEAR and SIGNIFICANT mission to inspire and motivate those to succeed who feel as though life's circumstances has disqualified them from possessing their rightful place in life.

The POWERFUL and DYNAMIC message that Cynthia passionately imparts to her audiences is summed up in just SIX words..."You CAN Be In Spite Of." The emphasis is on 'CAN.'

Cynthia is a licensed and ordained Minister who strategically meshes her motivational speaking and preaching skills to effectively encourage and inspire a variety of audiences.

Website: www.chowellmotivates.com
Instagram: https://www.instagram.com/chowellmotivates/
Twitter: @chowellmotiv8s
Contact: 352.440.3334

Journey to Strength with Endometriosis
By LeTysha N. Montgomery

My journey started fifteen years ago with a visit to the Ob-Gyn doctor. After explaining my symptoms and giving timelines, he said something that I have never heard of before-endometriosis. In my head, I am thinking, endo what? What is that? I had never heard that word in my life and little did I know that day that word would be used again later in my journey. Nor did I know that the word endometriosis would change my life forever.

Now, the doctor did give me a pamphlet about laparoscopy to surgically remove the endometriosis. I read the pamphlet and still have it to this day. They would cut an incision in my belly button and a few on my stomach as well. Really? I was in my mid-twenties at the time and really wanted a belly button ring. Cutting there wasn't something that I was okay with. I had never had surgery before and was scared. But none of that warranted surgery, did it? I had severe cramps, my periods weren't that heavy, and intercourse was painful, but none of the warranted surgery did it? Or was I just in denial about my situation and scared to go under the knife? Birth control pills were working for the cramps and the period. So, there wasn't really a reason to have surgery just to correct that one issue. Oh, how I wish I knew then what I know now, especially after 14 years of being on and off the pill and experiencing a failed IUD insertion.

Endometriosis (en-doe-me-tree-O-sis) is an often-painful disorder in which tissue similar to the tissue that normally lines the inside of your

uterus — the endometrium — grows outside your uterus.
Endometriosis most commonly involves your ovaries, fallopian tubes
and the tissue lining your pelvis. Information came from
mayoclinic.com

Laparoscopy (from Ancient Greek λαπάρα (lapara), meaning 'flank,
side', and σκοπέω (skopeo), meaning 'to see') is an operation
performed in the abdomen or pelvis using small incisions (usually 0.5–
1.5 cm) with the aid of a camera. The laparoscope aids diagnosis or
therapeutic interventions with a few small cuts in the abdomen.
Information came from Wikipedia

Endometriosis affects 1 in 10 women or anyone with female anatomy.

Fast forward to June 2019, the month that would begin to change my
life forever. I have a better tolerance for pain, but the second week of
June in 2019 was my breaking point. See, I thought I could struggle
through the right ovary pain like I had for the last two weeks. But that
night before I went to get checked out, the pain was way more intense.
I seriously thought my ovary would burst, or I was going to die of
extreme pain. So, I gave in and went to the Emergency Room, which
wasted about four hours of my life. And I was still in severe pain
because they never could get the IV in after four tries to give me oral
pain medication. I definitely won't be going to that Emergency Room
ever again in life. They gave me some medication that didn't help and
told me to follow up with an Ob-Gyn if the pain persisted. They
recommended an Ob-Gyn. I am thinking good; maybe I can get into
the doctor they recommended sooner than my own Ob-Gyn. Their
doctor ended up being a nightmare, just like the Emergency Room visit
had been. She couldn't find anything wrong with me but mentioned
that I could have endometriosis that has to be verified by a
laparoscopy. There is that word again-endometriosis. Little did I know
endometriosis would be used a lot from that day forward.

I still needed to see my doctor to figure out what this horrible pain was.
So, I called and, of course, I would have to wait until August. August
seemed like a lifetime away (two months), and my pain hadn't gotten

any better. I was assertive and told the scheduler that I needed a sooner appointment because I was in severe pain. It was at that moment; I became an advocate for myself and my health. I didn't realize that being an advocate would change my life. By advocating for myself, I did get a sooner appointment on July 8th. But this visit would be unlike any other that I ever had. You see, before that appointment, I knew what needed to be done, and I wasn't afraid anymore. I knew that I had to find the answer to my pain. So, on that day, I actually agreed to a laparoscopy to see if I had endometriosis.

Never in my wildest dream did I think having surgery would be my idea. But I knew my body and that it was crying out for help. That Emergency Room visit was a wake-up call to advocate for myself because I know my body best. Surgery was scheduled approximately a month later in August 2019. I was so scared about the surgery but knew it needed to be done. I read all I could about endometriosis and the surgery. I even watched YouTube videos about it and packed an overnight bag just in case, like instructed. I had no idea what I was in for but was headed full steam ahead. I remember asking all of my friends to pray for me. I remember one of my friends who works in the medical field was very helpful and informative. They told me what foods to eat post-op, what types of things to pack in my bag, and even what types of clothes work best. I had never had surgery like this before, so that information was so important.

Surgery day was here, and I was in a pretty good mood. I was finally ready to face my fears. I didn't really worry about the scars anymore because I was a warrior. Did I still want a belly button ring? Kinda. But I wanted to feel better and get an official diagnosis more. Was I nervous? Most definitely, but I didn't let it stop me from what I needed to do. I can't explain it exactly, but I came out of the operating room a different person than I was. I had a higher pain tolerance, was more in tune with my body, and had the belief that I could handle anything. I was a new person in some respects! The surgery went fantastic, my recovery went well, and I never took any pain medication post-op after being released.

In September 2019, I finally was diagnosed with endometriosis. It was a bittersweet day filled with many emotions- good and bad. It was good to finally know the diagnosis, but the details of the condition were still unknown. Endometriosis doesn't have a cure, and medication can help some people's pain. I really didn't want to be on medication. I was tired of the pill and just wanted to listen to my body. Honestly, the pill just masks your symptoms, so you forget about them. I am an endo warrior and don't want to mask my symptoms.

I feel like my endometriosis journey has taught me so many things. The most important is to advocate for myself. Secondly, I learned that I am stronger than any pain. And lastly, everything happens in its own time and own way. If I would have had the surgery any other time besides when I did, I wouldn't be doing what I am now. I am teaching others about endometriosis and advocating for themselves plus their health. Always trust your journey and yourself!!

Here are four ways for you to advocate for yourself and your health. I challenge you to use them!

1) Speak Up
You know your body better than anyone else. Don't be afraid to speak up and advocate for yourself- it might save your life.

2) Documentation
Write down your symptoms and the dates. See if there is a pattern and go over the details with your doctor.

3) Don't be afraid to get a second opinion
You know whether or not your doctor is taking your concerns seriously or not. Sometimes it takes a new perspective or a fresh set of eyes and ears to help you.

4)   *Don't Give Up*

Take the time to be persistent and never give up on yourself or your health.

LeTysha N. Montgomery

My name is LeTysha Montgomery. I am a jewelry designer, entrepreneur, speaker, author, educator, endometriosis advocate & podcaster.

Stand Out Style specializes in one-of-a-kind beaded jewelry in various styles & colors. I have sold my creations in retail stores & small businesses, showcased to a national chain buyer in Los Angeles, & been interviewed by a television station in Lawrence, KS. While selling at craft shows throughout the country, I have received several blue ribbons (Maker of Merit) & have been nominated for Top Accessory Designer of the Year.

I am a certified AmplifyHER national speaker who motivates & dares the audience to advocate for themselves & their health. My podcast about endometriosis is listened to all over the world. I was featured in Who's Who in Black Kansas City. I believe life goals are very important & always maintain a vision board.

www.instagram.com/stand_out_style
Standoutstyle.Storenvy.com
https://podcasts.apple.com/us/podcast/endometriosis-journey-to-butterfly/id1473744089?uo=4

The Sentence: The Day Justice was Silent
By Monica Morgan

"I should have kept on shooting," ran through my mind as I stood in the federal courtroom waiting for sentencing.

I stood tall and proud. I didn't know how else to stand, being a proponent of "image is everything." My hair was in my signature waved hairstyle; I wore a classy suit in my signature black; my signature red lipstick shone brightly on my lips. My outward demeanor was of the utmost confidence, my overall 'signature' look. Yet, newspapers later described me as looking as if I was dressed to go to my own funeral. So, they wished.

My charismatic, well-connected attorney, Steve Fishman, who was deemed one of the top criminal lawyers around, stood by my side. I felt confident, as this was his playground, and I'd heard he always played to win.

I looked up front at the diminutive figure who ironically held all the power. This was the judge who would decide whether or not I'd go to prison. In the beginning, there was a period when I felt he would be fair.

My lawyer had decided that I would not speak. Not speak? That's what I do; that's what I'm good at. No, I wouldn't condemn my husband.

No, unlike what some others were saying of him, I would not put it all on "the dead man."

"God has me, God has me," I affirmed in my head to help me feel on the inside, the way I presented on the outside.

My thoughts went back to the email that changed my life.

I was documenting an SBA event featuring the newly selected presidential appointee, head of the organization. As with many an assignment throughout my career, I was the official photographer.

Why had I even checked my email? A habit, of course. I scanned through the email from my lawyer, and it said I was being indicted as a co-defendant in a case. What? I read it over and over quickly several times. It had to be a mistake. It had to be a joke. I almost laughed. Soon though, it felt like the wind was being knocked out of me when I realized there was no punchline. All this was really happening. It was real.

I grabbed my camera and did what I only knew how to… take pictures and complete my assignment. I wished I had kept on shooting and never checked my email in the first place.

As soon as the event was over, I called my attorney after what seemed an eternity, and he explained the email. Yes, it was real. He told me that no one was going to come and arrest me (like I'd seen in so many movies), but that he couldn't keep it out of the news. The news?! I had to alert my family. I called my cousin Marla and explained the situation. She took it well and told me that I had her full support. I called a couple of close friends, and shared the news, receiving the same supportive response.

I had visions of tv cameras and microphones coming to surround me. I sat back in my car, turned on some of my favorite music, and attempted to relax. I'd always loved getting lost in music. Now, I actually needed to.

"Act, don't react." Those words filled my soul, and I smiled, thanking my grandfather for instilling that message in me as a child.

I knew what I would do. I put my car into gear and headed to Detroit's Chene Park; after all, there was a concert I was scheduled to cover. I made the conscious decision to continue to "do me" no matter what. I was determined to control my own narrative.

I gracefully covered the concert and remember someone asking, "Didn't I just see you on the news?" I smiled in answer and continued my work.

Then there began the endless texts and calls that I let voicemail handle. There was tremendous support despite what felt to me like my impending execution.

The next few months were filled with negative news coverage. I've since learned that I was "clickable," and news outlets needed that. I actually feel sorry for reporters who will compromise seeking the truth and write anything to earn their paycheck. I wonder how they can actually look in the mirror after tossing objectivity aside to simply keep a job. I stopped consuming the news, as reporters seemed to be creating the narrative any way they wanted. So, when friends called to see if I was "ok" after reading, hearing, or seeing more stories, I countered with, "I have no idea what's being said. What is going on with me?"

I continued with my normal routine; to show up with grit and grace amid the bad press and the government trying to break and finish me.

Perhaps if I had allowed them to break me, I wouldn't have had to go down the path they had obviously set for me.

You may read this as something that could never happen to you. If you are alive operating in America, it could happen to you. Our criminal justice system is a formidable opponent, and careers are made when they are successful in beating you. I imagined my career and everything I'd worked for and built over my lifetime was now finished with this sentence.

Many have asked how I survived; how I continued to stay and look strong. I realized that resilience is not innate but something that you can learn. Something you may have to learn.

Resilience is how I'm still standing. The following ten steps were instilled in me by God to grow through what I experienced.

Pray incessantly and have faith. God will hear you. He may not give you the answer you want, but He will respond.

Visualize the bigger picture and see yourself emerging from your trials and tribulations with grace.

Find an affirmation that makes you feel better.

Act instead of react.

Image is everything. Show them who you are.

Listen to music that uplifts and makes you want to dance.

Dance as if it's all that matters.

Spend time with people who support, encourage, and inspire you.

Have a trusted friend or mentor who you can reach out to 24/7.

Help others. Realize that your struggle, whatever it may be, will provide you with the experience to help -perhaps even save- someone else.

I had already endured so much, being accidentally shot at close range by a 45 caliber Desert Eagle handgun, and the bullet exiting one-half centimeter from my spine, then losing my soulmate -my husband- to pancreatic cancer while we were still just newlyweds. And now, this.

I didn't think I could endure anymore, yet, God had me. That was the affirmation that kept me going, "God has me," and I believed that with every fiber of my being.

The prosecutor said that all of my life's good works and accomplishments were even more reason to make an example of me. How that notion made sense, I'll never know, and to this day, I couldn't tell you. So, the judge sentenced me to eighteen months in a federal prison camp for women.

I remained calm, yet a myriad of emotions went through me. None good. And I felt it through my entire being. So much so, by this point, I began to have thoughts of ending my life. It had gotten to be too much. I was so tired. Eventually, I pulled it together. I realized if I did that, they'd win. They'd be able to write and finish my narrative.

A few hours after the sentencing, I boarded a plane to a speaker's conference in Texas. While in flight, I had a mental meltdown with God. I was angry with Him. Didn't I do everything that I was supposed to? I had believed He had me, and I knew those weapons formed against me wouldn't prosper. So, why had he let them win? Why had he given the haters what they wanted? Why had HE sentenced me to this?

On November 5, 2018, I self-surrendered to a Satellite Camp in Lexington, Kentucky. I smiled as I entered, knowing then that God had a plan, and He had me. After what seemed like a sabbatical in a third world country, I walked out those same doors and flew home thirteen months later. Now, I'm here, back among the world, among you.

I came to realize that God had me all along and hadn't let go. There is no manmade sentencing that overrides that. He had -and has- plans for me. So, I'm still standing, more experienced, more confident. I'm prepared to do even more for others. Living and standing tall through whatever comes is how I truly "finish" this sentence.

Monica Morgan

Monica Morgan's drive to tell visual stories has made her undisputedly one of the world's most well-known, highly accomplished, sought-after, African-American photographers.

Morgan's WireImage.com contract establishes international access to her images for editors, entertainment, and news media.

With a lifetime of world-class historical and celebrity photography as a backdrop, Morgan ascended from the Detroit-area, gracing the world stage, teaching, and speaking to audiences from all walks of life, sharing from her own life lessons.

Morgan's story features personal tragedy and turmoil, turbulent events making her ever-determined to speak to and for those in need of inspiration and advocacy.

"It's the ability to capture moments that make history. . . those moments, through the lens, that make stories worth telling," she said.

She tells those stories globally, as she views the world, love, and life through HER lens.

www.MonicaMorganSpeaks.com
Monica@MonicaMorganSpeaks.com

Becoming Strong in the Midst of Life's Storms
By Sandra V. Phillips

"She's DOA; let's check the other vehicles." This is what I heard almost 23 years ago. It all started with a terrible multicar accident;- hands down the worst bumper car ride of my life. An otherwise peaceful ride was interrupted with a sudden jolting, spinning, and flipping. The cacophony of metal scraping was shortly replaced by a clear voice, speaking so close I felt I could reach out and touch their lips. I couldn't respond. My body was frozen, unable to move or make a sound. I laid as motionless as the seat I occupied, only able to listen to my surroundings. I wondered, 'How can I let them know I'm alive?' A small muscle twitch, an audible breath, anything. Anything to let them know I was still here. You see, I didn't know how it felt to be dead. I had to ask myself if I were truly dead, would I still be able to hear? My cognitive functions and senses seemed intact, elevated even. I started mentally assessing my physical capabilities, starting with my lower extremities. My toes wouldn't wiggle, my knees couldn't bend, and my hips dared not shake.

Moving upwards, I found my hands and arms also refused their orders to move. My assessment was not over, but I must admit I lessened the pace, unsure how I would handle the complete results. For a person who shouldn't be breathing, I took in the deepest breath ever and tried to force a sound to escape my lips. Fruitless, just as suspected, I couldn't make the tiniest of utterances. On to the final part of my assessment. My eyelids had relaxed into a shut state; tried as I might, I couldn't open them. I must be dead. As if possible, I closed my eyes more and began surrendering to death.

Fear did not touch me; instead, there was a calmness of peace that fell over me. I couldn't understand the meaning behind it, but it felt purposeful and very intentional. Why this calmness? Why am I not freaking out? It hit me suddenly; I had this huge OMG moment. I was alone in the car! My baby girl was not with me. I had left her with friends, which was not part of the original plan- well, not my plan anyway. My soul cried out in euphonious sounds of the highest praise, "Hallelujah." My immobile body began to dance like David giving praises unto God for His protection. This moment gave new meaning and perspective to the scripture, 'In everything give thanks,' 1 Thessalonians 5:18. I know some of you are thinking, 'Praises for protection, but Sis, weren't you assumed to dead on arrival?' Yes, but I still felt blessed that my child was unharmed. It was with that knowledge and understanding that my daughter was safe, that my whole body, from the crown of my head to the soles of my feet, exhaled with a sigh of relief and gratitude. I felt complete in total serenity and tranquility- something I have never experienced at this magnitude. Could this be the peace I've heard and read about in the Word? Yes, it is that 'Peace, far beyond human understanding' Philippians 4:7. It is well within my soul.

But, God! It's not over until God gives the final say so. I opened my eyes slightly only to be blinded by a piercing beam of light. Blinking, I reopened them wider only to be taken aback by what I saw. Bright, ruby-red blood flowed like a river down the side of my car window. Again, fear did not touch me; instead, I felt saved. Another voice came to me, "I'm going to get you out, ma'am, don't worry." I was removed from the car, still unable to move my lower body, by a nurse and a trucker. The paramedics who initially declared me DOA came rushing over and started taking my vital signs. They asked me repeatedly over and over about some numbers but assumed I had a head injury. One of the two voices I heard earlier was an off-duty nurse who recognized my repetitions as a telephone number to the elementary school where my sons were waiting for me to pick them up. She made contact with the school and my spouse regarding the accident. The other voice belonged to the truck driver who had stopped to lend assistance, breaking his hand on my car window in the process- that explained the blood. I would later search for these two without leads only to find that no one for the accident scene or hospital had any recollection of them.

An ambulance rushed me to the hospital, where I would soon learn of my injuries. Despite my earlier assessments, I thought I was only banged up and a bit bruised, but the reality caught me off guard, and I found the news unbelievable. "Ms. Phillips, we need to speak with you about a few things." The emergency room physician's team told me. I knew whatever they had to tell me must have been serious if it required a whole team of physicians to share this information. Their faces were laden with concern and confusion- another indicator of the gravity of the situation. The lead physician approached my bed and asked, "Ms. Phillips, do you know what happened to you today?." "Yes," I replied, "I was involved in a car accident." He appeared shocked for a moment then hummed with a sigh, "Can you tell me, Ms. Philips, how you are feeling?" I remember my response like it was yesterday. Injecting levity into this serious conversation, I took in a deep breath and chuckled, "I'm okay, but I've had better days." I could tell something was going on but couldn't put my finger on it, and the physicians were playing 21 questions rather than getting to the point. The lead physician pressed on with his interrogation, unaware of how badly I wanted to have him thrown out of my room. "Ms. Phillips, what's your pain level on a scale of 1-10?" My response of "Around 2 or 3" was not the correct or expected answer to give. The physicians huddled together, one of them leaving the room before quickly returning. My patience was gone. I needed to know what was going on.

"Just tell me," I said in a firm voice. Finally, they broke the news to me. I was told my left hip was broken, and my pelvis was crushed.

Crushed. I couldn't absorb anything being said immediately following that Word. I saw the physician's lips move, but no sound came. I thought it was a mistake. It must be a mistake. I asked them to double-check the medical records to confirm it was me. It was. I now had questions of my own, "Why aren't I in excruciating pain?" He started to answer, but I cut him off, "What type of pain medication did you give me?" His response didn't make any sense to me, "I just had it double checked, but none." I was yelling now, "Well, give me some!" Didn't he understand? My pelvis was crushed. He asked again, "Are you in pain?" I had to be honest, as unbelievable as it was, I replied, "No, not really." No one could understand. There was no medical reason why my pain level was almost non-existent. One of the young residents moved forward, leaning over towards me to say, "The blood of Jesus covered you, Ms. Phillips."

This was the first day of the rest of my life. My journey of long-suffering and mighty reward has begun, and there was no looking back. The road I travel has not always been easy but has been a story of trust and triumph. In the years to follow, I have faced three hip replacement surgeries, blood clots, venous stasis ulcers, hemorrhaging, and a diagnosis of chronic kidney disease. There are days I still struggle, but He has prepared me. I realized I was in a spiritual workout for my life. My challenges and struggles are my barbells of endurance and faith. I had to stand on God's Word to literally stand again. I utilized the Word as a survival guide and coined the term "Faith Factors": (here's a few)

- **Job Faith:** Keep your eyes on God and don't turn around; press on and don't let possessions, things, and people create a barrier between you and God. He will give it back 2-fold.

- **Jericho Faith:** Just because you don't see God working doesn't mean He's not. Be obedient and watch the walls come tumbling down in your life.

- **Eagle Faith:** The book of Isaiah speaks of mounting up on wings like an eagle. Be patient and wear those wings, God created to fly above, beneath, and more importantly, through a storm.

Through it all, I became strong amid life's storms. Because He is the great I am, I am still standing.

Sandra V. Phillips

Sandra V. Phillips is a licensed professional counselor in Georgia with over 15 years of experience. She also holds Certified Alcohol and Drug Abuse Counselor II (& International), DOT-Substance Abuse Professional, National Certified Counselor, and Certified Professional Counselor Supervisor credentials. She received both master's degrees from Troy University. Her private practice group, Transformation Behavioral Health, LLC www.transformation3cs.com, provides counseling services to a diverse population. Ms. Phillips is a proud Star Behavioral Provider for our military personnel, veterans, and their dependents. She is also a children's book author. As the founder of a nonprofit organization, Transformation Training Institute, Inc. www.transformationtraininginc.com. she commits to providing low cost and free training on multicultural, diversity, and behavioral health issues. Ms. Phillips believes true transformation comes through the renewing of your mind.

She is available for speaking engagement as well as a training facilitator. Best contact method: sandravphillips1@gmail.com

Knocked Out But...
By Carla Rascoe

You never knew which way things would go with my father, but he seemed pleasant today despite his insecurities around higher education. When he pulled up, I jumped into his shiny maroon Jaguar. Midas Touch blasted through the expensive speaker system, and we sped away.

We made small talk about my grades and job. He inquired if I was "seeing some boy" and jammed his parental nuggets in the twenty minutes it took to get to campus. "You can take yourself to dinner and a movie," he told me for the 100th time. I guess it was his way of reminding me of my worth.

He parked, and we headed towards the admissions office. As we joined the long line wrapped around the building, I prayed that Daddy could last long enough. We laughed about old times and chatted about the latest fashions he copped on his recent New York trip. I was glad that kept us busy enough until we reached the front of the line.

I registered for four of the five classes I wanted. The last one, which I needed, was already full. The admissions counselor whispered that the professor had about five extra spaces available. Then she gave me an override form. She scribbled the name of the professor and the building and room number on a sticky.

"Take this over there now, and you can probably still get one of those spots." She winked.

I made my way to the building as fast as I could with Daddy in tow. He seemed paranoid about the counselor whispering to me.

"What was that about?" he asked. I didn't want him to get loud.

"She was saying that if the teacher over here signs off, I can probably still get in the class."

There were three other students and their parents ahead of us when we finally found the room. This was one of those classes that was only offered in the fall, so if you missed it, you were almost guaranteed to be graduating a semester late.

"We gotta stand in another line?" Daddy asked. He seemed agitated.

I shushed him and rolled my eyes.

Daddy shot me a look like he was about to check me but decided against it.

I prayed that he would let me do most of the talking when it was our turn to talk to the professor.

"Hi, how are you?" The Afrocentric teacher asked pleasantly.

"Hi," I smiled back. I knew instantly I'd like her class.

I handed her the override form.

"What was that you gave her?" Daddy asked suspiciously. Dude was lunchin.

Reviewing the form, the teacher noticed that I would be a transfer student. "What school did you attend before?" she asked.

Before I could answer, my father butted in.

"Her ass is transferring here from North Carolina," he blurted out. "Had a scholarship and all, but she got down there showing off and messed that up. Now we here doing this," he continued.

"Daddy," I whispered, trying to get him to be quiet.

"I'm the father here," he piped up. He was in full out rare form and was going to make it known that even with an education, no one was better than him.

I managed to say thank you as I snatched the completed form. I fast-walked to the hallway.

Angry and embarrassed, I wondered why he couldn't act like the other fathers.

"So, you think you gonna get to this school and think you better than me?" he asked as soon as he hit the hallway.

I'm sure the people still in the classroom heard him.

"Shhhh," I plead with him.

"No, you don't tell me what to do. I'm the father here, and don't you forget it." He angrily charged towards me. I was filled with disbelief as his chest puffed up, and he balled his fist tighter with every step.

Oh, hell naw. He was about to fight me like a nigga on the street.

Suddenly I felt a strong blow. My right jaw cracked as my head flew to the left. I couldn't believe a father would punch his daughter this way.

I only allowed a few seconds for heartbreak then I began fighting him back. If he wasn't gonna be a father, I wouldn't be a daughter.

We rumbled for what must have been ten, fifteen minutes. I had him on the floor until he crawled away from me in his ripped shirt. He had a busted lip that was slightly bleeding. I noticed him holding his right leg and limping when he finally struggled to his feet. I stood up and brushed myself off. He was obviously more tattered than I was.

"Take the bus home bitch," he spat as he threw a few dollars on the ground and started to leave. I saw the false pride returning as his back got a little straighter. He tried not to hobble away as he tucked in his torn shirt.

I grabbed the money, my big trunk earrings, and my sunglasses. I guess when my father was channeling Mike Tyson, they slid across the hallway. I headed towards the lady's room.

I made it to the nearest stall before the tears came. I cried and cried until I couldn't breathe, shedding a mixture of love and hate, anger and acceptance, embarrassment, and pride, all mixed with shame. I let it all come forth right then and there.

My soul ached as I tried to wrap my mind around what just happened. I thought that a father was supposed to be an example of love. I think my father got intimidated by being on a college campus. And I think as proud as he was of me, he was more ashamed of himself, and it was all too much. I allowed myself those few minutes to grieve.

"Come on," the Spirit called out to me. "Yes, that was some crazy stuff," He agreed, "but you came here to register for classes."

"Come on," I heard it clearly as it led me to the sink. With each step, I heard Him whisper, "You got this."

Believing Him, I found the strength to wash my face. When I looked in the mirror, I could tell my jaw was crooked. Bravely I took a deep breath, and on the count of three, I snapped it back into place. It hurt like hell.

I took a deep sigh as I walked out of the bathroom and to the financial aid office. Daddy offered to pay the bill so I wouldn't have any loans, but I quickly accepted that was over. Loans it would have to be.

I stopped at the payphone along the way to call my mother.

"Hey, Ma. Can you come and pick me up from the school?"

"Yeah, I was already on my way. Your father just called me, are you alright?" she sounded frantic.

"Yes, Ma, I'm fine."

"He said that y'all got into a fight," she still sounded shook up.

"Yeah, we did. He got up here showing off. I tried to shush him because I have to go to school with these people, and he went off."

My mother sighed. "Just wait outside. I will be there to get you shortly."

"How bout I come out as soon as I finish registering?"

My mother let out a relieved laugh.

"Yeah. I'm not gonna let anything derail me from the reason I'm here."

"That's my daughter," my mother said. "I'll be there as soon as I can."

As soon as I finished, I got into my mother's car, and she gave me a long, deep hug, which I fell into. We broke apart, flashing each other a resilient smile.

"I just love you," she said, marveling at the fact that I handled my business despite the circumstances.

"You don't even look like you been in a fight, but then again, your father did say you whipped his ass like a man."

Oddly, my father proudly, lovingly repeated this story at family gatherings for years. My takeaways from this are:

1. **Various things in life will happen but we can still be successful despite it.**
   Even though he could never voice it, my father was proud that even in adversity I could handle myself and take care of my business.

2. **God is so loving that He meets us right where we are.**
   I had just encountered one of the worse experiences of my life and was in a low place in a campus bathroom, but God still saw fit to be with and encourage me.

3. **We really can do all things through Christ who strengthens us.**

In this instance: I found the strength to pull through and not fall apart, I was still able to have my wits about me to continue the school registration process, and I found the ability to forgive.

Carla Rascoe

Carla Rascoe is a Federal Government Professional residing in the Washington Dc Area. She is a mother of two responsible, brilliant, amazing young men who are both in their early 20s. A resilient and smart young woman, she possesses both a Bachelor of Science and a Master of Social Work Degree. Called to empower, support, encourage, and lead, she will be releasing her own story of triumph and challenge if you want to know more.

She can be contacted at crrascoe@gmail.com for engagements.

Ignorance of Arrogance: 17 at 17ish Project

By Robin Richardson

EVEN as I am writing this chapter, I had to stop and read my' stop tripping and function life scripture!' "Trust in the Lord with all your heart; do not depend on your own understanding. Seek His will in all you do, and He will show you which path to take." Proverbs 3:5-6 NLT

I am Still Standing! Through it all, I have learned to trust the Lord for direction. Unlike GPS, HIS directions are always correct! Seriously, I have written my own directions many times over, which is why so many journeys were circles! Trusting God has given me the ability to encourage and inspire others.

The title of this chapter is "Ignorance of Arrogance." For example, All of my life, one of my favorite movies the Charles Dickens, 'A Christmas Carol.' Mr. Scrooge! I love this story because it always shows the 'heart opening' moment for Scrooge. However, year after year, I would still be surprised that he was so "ignorant of his own arrogance"!

Where I'm coming from: You see, I became a mother at the ripe old age of 17. I must say it is a lifetime experience! I have no regrets about being a Mom! My children are the biggest gifts in my life! Although, being a 17-year-old parent is certainly not easy and definitely not recommended (it really isn't God's plan). However, it happens, and when it does, we need to be ready to support, not ostracize or even worse, pretend they don't exist! What do I mean by that? I know some people will be offended by that statement, saying "not me," but it's true. It's usually prefaced with things like, 'you had that baby, now take care of it,' or the 'nothing you do is right' attitude.

As I matured, I began sharing experiences with friends who were also teen moms. Now that the children are adults, I realized I dealt with way more than being a single teen mom. Specifically, the arrogance that came with the stigma of being a teen mother. The bigger problem is most people are ignorant of their behavior and sometimes in your own circle! Surely this way of thinking can be attributed to much in life, classism, racism, educational hierarchy, etc. That's for later; right now, my area of focus is parenthood circa age 17. Consciously or unconsciously, it makes the situation worse! Imagine this:

What would happen if we nurture, support, and guide teen parents by sharing experiences, our no's & don'ts, and our yes & do's?

More on Scrooge... There's a point in the movie where Scrooge is approached by some Good Samaritans asking for a donation to an orphanage. He didn't want to help and asked them, "Are there no prisons, are there no workhouses?" See, in his mind, he believed that poverty was supposed to be punished by imprisonment. Surely poverty was criminal, right? However, this is something that we all need to understand emphatically. The same attitude can often be perpetuated toward teen parents. Side Swipe: "Be aware of arrogance, so it does not seep into your soul and become a part of your mental DNA." Meaning most people do not even recognize how much arrogance affects their lives and decisions they make for themselves and their children.

First, to be Arrogant is to have an exaggerated sense of one's own importance or abilities. Second, to be ignorant is to be lacking knowledge of information or awareness about a particular thing. Y'all, let's persevere in becoming aware of when we are arrogant toward others. More importantly, when someone else's exaggerated sense of importance affects our life's decisions and self-worth. It is for the welfare of our next generations. I am not saying that every time you give or get advice about something (solicited or not), it's arrogance. Here's the thing, is it being approached from a place of support or arrogance? It also means that 'we' have to be careful of our giving and receiving criticisms to and of others because it may not be constructive even when the advice is correct. The attitude could quite possibly be an expression of a superiority complex. Construction builds up, arrogance tears down. If you can criticize without the construction of an action – revealing a step to take to build, then you are ignorant of your own arrogance. "Criticism is only constructive when it builds."

Surely you can see the theme here. I want to identify those areas where we are ignorant of our own arrogance and how it can affect those we influence. Please understand I am not just pointing fingers at 'you,' but at us, as people, acting out in our human self-importance. Sideswipe: God requires humility from us. Now, you may say this is just your opinion, and you'd be right. I don't claim any degrees in this. What I do claim is over 40 years of personal learning and growing through a watchful study of people, interactions & experiences.

It began many years ago when, as a young mother, I realized certain perceptions about me were merely assumptions born out of arrogance. It was 20 years ago, almost to the date in 2000, when I began to write this book, 'the first time.'

At that time, I recognized something about the people around me personally and professionally. I realized that many of them didn't even notice they were exhibiting the level of arrogance they had toward me. Oh yeah, sideswipe: "Keep a check on your circle of influence. Don't bring people into your mental house that belong in the backyard!"

Moving on- At times, I would get irritated and even defensive because of the 'it's your fault attitudes, and to some degree, that is true. However, we can't get pregnant by ourselves, but I digress.

In the meantime, I noticed that conversations were different with me than with my counterparts who were married. As if my children deserved less support or should be pitied because I was not married. Ok, how arrogant! The truth is many of us have preconceived ideas about others, and in many cases, the only difference is they had the sex but didn't get pregnant or got pregnant and didn't have the baby or hid the pregnancy, had the baby but didn't raise the child. Most of the time, the actions are being justified by disguising them as honesty. When the arrogance comes, it's justified by saying things like, "I'm just being honest..." Please be honest about your honesty!

Please don't get me wrong; we are not about to do a deep intrusion into 'victim valley' here. Absolutely not! This is not about what someone said or did to us and blaming. It is about how those words and actions affected us and how we can use it to positively change our own course of action. As well as be a positive impact in the life of someone navigating the same course. Let's recognize the attitudes and perceptions that shaped our abilities as parents, whether positive or negative. It will cause you to focus on the best possible encouragement for our children. God allows experiences in our lives to help someone else amid their experience.

Story Begins: The Mountain Retreat...

It's Friday, Memorial Day weekend 1978. I'm sitting on the front porch looking out of the window, hoping my boyfriends' car comes down the street. Surely, he'd want to come over this weekend because my family went to the mountains to a retreat. Now, I wasn't asked to go to the retreat; it wasn't even a consideration. You see, I was 17 years old, seven months pregnant – and not married. Looking back, I should have been the first one they dragged out of the door!

I was in the beginning stage of that uncomfortable wobble walk, constantly moving from place to place from the living room to the porch to the kitchen... all weekend. All weekend I sat by the window watching and waiting, occasionally calling, "are you coming?" the response was always yes, but the answer was always no. It took me years to realize how jammed up I was about that weekend, about that season, about attitudes on every side. I stayed alone that weekend, why, because I was 17 years old and seven months pregnant with the pregnancy that would soon bring me to death's door...

"I am Still Standing" and hoping to inspire those women navigating motherhood beginning in their teen years with "The 17 at 17ish Project". It is a forum where gathered thoughts and shared experiences help to smooth the course.

Look for the "Ignorance of Arrogance" book in the Spring of 2021!

Robin Richardson

Robin Richardson is a well-accomplished professional with more than 20 years of administrative & event coordination experience. She is currently the CEO and Owner of Events Assured LLC, an administrative & event services company. She is a consummate professional dedicated to making the load lighter for busy executives. Ms. Richardson is an effective gatekeeper supporting the processes of efficient business operations. She is also embarking on her heart passion endeavor, the '17 at 17ish Project'. This project aims to foster a supportive & encouraging environment for women who embarked on motherhood circa the crucial age of 17 years old. This will be accomplished through information gathering of shared experiences and resources, resulting in conclaves and masterclasses. For more information regarding administrative or event services, click the link below: www.eventsassuredplan.com. You can find the 'The 17 at 17ish Project' on Facebook.

What Was Lost
By Nikki A. Rogers

December 29, 2016, started as a great day – my husband, 4-year-old son, and I slept in after our midnight arrival at my mother-in-law's house in Chapel Hill, NC. We had a late breakfast, and I spent the afternoon finishing Christmas shopping for relatives I expected to see at our annual New Year's Day dinner party. Then, it was off to date night with friends to watch the latest Star Wars movie.

Three-quarters of the way into the movie, I realized I had missed several calls from my sister-in-law. My immediate thought was something had happened to my brother or one of the kids. I stepped out to return her call. She answered and asked with urgency, "Have you talked to your mom?" My mom? Why was she asking about my mom?

"No, I haven't talked to her today. She's coming tomorrow." My mom and I were going to shop and prep for New Year's Day dinner when she arrived.

My sister-in-law started to cry and said that they had been calling and knocking on my mom's door for a while. Her car was in front of the house, but she was not answering. Logic kicked in, coupled with a sense of hope – had they called 9-1-1? Could someone get into the house through a window? Maybe she's just hurt or not feeling well? That sense of hope sustained me as I waited for her to return my call.

She soon called back with the life-altering news that my brothers and I had lost our mom.

My brain refused to accept this new reality. I felt sick to my stomach, and I cried as we made it back to the house to pack an overnight bag. We decided to leave our son with his (now) only grandmother. On the 2 ½ hour drive to my hometown, I alternatively cried, screamed, rationalized, and prayed that the news was simply untrue. My mother had recently celebrated her 67th birthday, and she was fine when we talked the day before. This didn't make sense. But it was true – she had died of respiratory failure at home earlier that day. By the time I arrived, the house was empty, but it felt like my mom was out running errands. The Christmas tree lights were on – my mom loved Christmas – and there were gifts and shopping bags all around, and ingredients for a red velvet cake on the counter.

On New Year's Day, instead of celebrating with family and friends, my brother and I were at the funeral home making final arrangements. I had barely slept. We brought in photos for my mom's hairstyle, her favorite lipstick, jewelry, shoes, and a garnet red and black dress as her final outfit. The funeral director showed us a casket comparable to the one chosen for our dad in December 2005, and we selected the color we thought our mom would like. It was surreal, as my brother and I sat in the director's office in front of her massive desk, calmly discussing the arrangements. Inside, I was screaming and slowly falling to pieces.

The next five days until the funeral were a blur, coordinating with the pastor, arranging for the eulogy minister and program participants, writing the obituary, ordering a casket spray, confirming the burial plot location, and figuring out what to wear. I also had to explain death to my 4-year-old, who kept asking about Grandma. I remember a few details from the funeral service – the packed church, the eloquent, rousing eulogy that would have made my mom proud, and sitting on the front pew of the church with the funeral attendant handing me tissues. At the repast, I saw all my girlfriends who had come to pay their respects – my mom always did love my friends. It was a small glimmer of cheer amidst the grief and sadness that was beginning to settle into my soul.

I returned to work a week later but was not ready to deal with grief. You see, grief is the worst kind of bully. It leaves you alone for a while, then sucker punches you at work, in your car, while shopping, or in the shower. You can't dodge it, nor do you get a warning sign. I tried to resist, then realized that I had to take the hit, breathe through it, and wake up the next day. Grief was ever-present as the weeks went by. I cried every day. It felt like I was standing in the ocean at high tide, with the waves of grief bowling me over when I least expected it. I was struggling to reach equilibrium before being sucked under. When the waves of grief were too high, I took days off work and stayed in bed. I felt sad, angry, cheated, robbed, and depressed.

The shattered pieces of my life crashed down as I realized the extent of my loss. I had lost my mom and so much more:

- My mentor and example as a mother, sister, aunt, wife, and leader.

- My inspiration who was always involved in church and the community.

- My mirror who reflected my future physical appearance.

- My harshest critic who inoculated me against the outside world.

- My biggest cheerleader who celebrated my every success.

- My new-found friend who I genuinely enjoyed spending time with as an adult.

- My son's Grandma who was the direct connection to our southern roots and family legacy.

I felt untethered and had so many questions. How could I now exist as a motherless daughter? When someone has been with you from before your first breath, how do you live without them? From whom would I continue to learn about being a mother as my son grew? And selfishly, who would make the oft-requested red velvet cake for future family gatherings?

As the months went by, my husband took on more and more household duties. I barely managed to shower each day, enveloped in a cloud of sadness that turned into a full-blown depression, manifesting as mopey irritability. I would awake from nightmares in which I was wandering around searching for my mom. I was tenuously hanging on to my sanity, and loved ones advised me to see a therapist. Instead, I resigned from my job and used my sadness as fuel to start a business. That wasn't enough – I felt like the shards of my shattered self were stabbing me. I was emotionally bleeding over my entire life – as a wife, mother, sister, friend, and new entrepreneur. I was angry about the financial and administrative burden of managing my mother's estate. I was exhausted and broken from the weight of sorrow and wanted the pain to stop. I finally went to therapy. It was helpful to talk to a neutral party about my feelings of sadness, anger, fear, abandonment, and at times, despair. I learned that I had to remodel my life around the grief rather than letting it become my life.

Four years later, I am still standing, aware of the grief that swirls around at low tide, ever-present but no longer overpowering. While I lost my mom, I gained a new appreciation for life. I found the courage to become a full-time entrepreneur. I discovered strength and resilience that will support me as I face future personal and professional challenges. I am still a work in progress, reimagining a future that does not include my mom, keeping her memory alive for my son, and leveraging the lessons she taught me to channel future growth.

If you are struggling in the ocean of grief over the loss of a loved one, I offer these lessons from my experience:

1. **Identify, discuss, and process all the emotions you are feeling** – sadness, anger, fear, disgust, distress, abandonment, worry, despair, relief, numbness – all feelings are relevant and deserve at least momentary attention.

2. **Write it down** – document your feelings, trigger points, and reactions to memories, people, and situations. These can all provide clues for the healing process.

3. **Talk to a professional.** Don't let the loss of your loved one overshadow your future. If grief is overwhelming, talk to a counselor or therapist about all the emotions and begin to live again.

4. **Avoid comparing your grieving process to others.** Everyone's process is different, based on their relationship, emotional state, and life circumstances.

5. **Create new traditions that honor your loved one and build new memories for everyone.**

6. **Be patient and gentle with yourself.** There is no set timeframe to complete the grieving process and get back to "normal." You have been forever transformed by loss. Lean into the new version of yourself that emerges.

7. **Develop an estate plan and organize important documents.** Reduce the burden on loved ones by ensuring your affairs are in order and providing guidance on your final wishes.

8. **Most importantly – find something to celebrate each day and enjoy the gift of life.**

Nikki A. Rogers

Nikki A. Rogers is a management consultant, transformation strategist, and business coach with 20+ years' experience in organizational change management, strategic planning, and project management across multiple industries.

Nikki believes life is too short not to do what you love and that controlling your time is the ultimate freedom. She is passionate about helping entrepreneurs build sustainable companies and supports business owners in developing the mindset, strategy, systems, and connections to create financial independence and generational wealth.

Nikki is an alumna of North Carolina A&T State University and UNC - Chapel Hill, and a certified Project Management Professional (PMP®) with graduate certificates in leadership development and change management. She is the CEO of The Bladen Group, Chief Strategist of Nikki Rogers, Inc., and host of the Women Thriving in Business podcast.

You can connect with Nikki via LinkedIn linkedin.com/in/nikki-rogers or on Instagram: @NikkiRogersOfficial.

Bullied From Second Grade To Sixth Grade In The New York School System

By Brenda Sawyer

"For the weapons of our warfare are not carnal, but mighty through God to the pulling down of strong holds."
2 Corinthians 10:4 (KJV)

"No weapon that is formed against thee shall prosper; and every tongue that shall rise against thee in judgment thou shalt condemn. This is the heritage of the servants of the Lord, and their righteousness is of me, saith the Lord."
Isaiah 54:17 (KJV)

Yes, we live in a world where the weapons are real and form daily but will not prosper against us. Why? Because this is the promise of my Father God that I have stood on as a child and still stand on today as an adult. Does it make you ever wonder why school bullying still happens to this day? Well, I was curious and decided to look up "school bullying" in the dictionary. "School bullying" is characterized as a type of bullying that occurs in any educational setting. For an act to be considered bullying, it must meet certain criteria; this includes hostile intent, imbalance of power, repetition, distress, and provocation. Wow! Just thinking about it makes me wonder why anyone at that age would want to have that much power and control over someone. I can remember being "picked on" and ridiculed by some of my classmates from the time I entered school until the bell rang at three o'clock.

Coming from a Christian family, I was taught morals and mutual respect for everyone, especially adults. Unfortunately, respect was not always reciprocated to me by some of my peers and, surprisingly, by some of my African American teachers. Yes, I can even remember my teachers embarrassing me and talking down to me in front of the whole class. Was I missing something here? I thought that my teachers were supposed to teach and build up my self-esteem as a black child, not try to tear me down. It felt like I was being bullied by my teachers as well. The bullying started in second grade, with three of my classmates, Jean, Ema, and Mary, who were supposed to be my friends. No matter how hard I tried to be friendly towards them, they would try to start a fight for no reason. Ema, would sometimes pull my hair, step on my new shoes, and knock me down. Jean, the ringleader, used to push me into Mary to start a fight. In my Christian household, I was taught not to fight. Every time this happened, I wanted to tell my teacher Mrs. Farrow but was afraid of the after-school repercussions. I remember telling my parents I didn't like school anymore and didn't want to return. Of course, being concerned parents, they advised me the next time it happened to tell Mrs. Farrow.

The next time I was bullied, I told Mrs. Farrow, and instead of trying to resolve the issue, she just ignored me and told me to stop acting like a baby. That same day, Jean, Mary, and Ema jumped me and beat me up after school. My parents were furious and decided to meet and talk to the girls' parents, thinking that might make a difference. The bullying did subside for about a week but started right back up again. My parents finally decided to meet and discuss the matter with Mrs. Farrow but to no avail. When my teacher made the "kids will be kids" statement, my parents became livid and decided to discuss the matter with the principal, Mrs. Tucker. There was an elephant in the room, but no one wanted to solve or address the problem. My parents requested a room transfer in the middle of the school year, which did seem to help somewhat. Since my school P.S. 103 never expelled students, I still came in contact with my bullies almost every day.

Can you believe nothing was done to resolve the issue? My parents told me to ignore and stay away from them, which was almost impossible to do.

One night I can remember crying until I made myself sick. I was so hurt and upset that I never wanted to return to school again. That night I started questioning God and asking Him, "Why me?" I was so angry that I wanted God to punish them for hurting me. However, I remembered the Bible verse, Matthew 5:44, which told me to love my enemies and pray for those who despitefully use me. Having a long talk with my parents about me loving my enemies gave me a change of heart. So, I prayed and asked God to help me love, forgive Jean, Ema, and Mary and to protect me from them. I was always taught to pray and knew that God would answer in His own time. Now I know prayer works because although I was still being bullied throughout sixth grade, it wasn't happening as much anymore.

I think God has a funny way of working things out sometimes because right before the end of sixth grade, I was beginning to heal from the hurt and pain of being bullied all those years. I can thank God the bullying eventually stopped, and we were on the road to building a friendship with each other. Was it the fact that we were getting older and preparing to enter middle school? I still don't know to this day, but I know that as we began to mature through life, we found out that we had much more in common than we knew. Jean and I found out that we celebrated our birthdays on the same day, December sixteenth. So, we never forgot each other's birthday. Ema and Mary started attending my same church; we even sang in the choir together. I know God was behind the scenes working everything out for our good. Romans 8:28 (KJV)

As my life began to unfold, and I blossomed into maturity, I knew that God had a much greater plan for me. One of my favorite Scriptures in the Bible is Jeremiah 29:11, which says, "For I know the thoughts that I think toward you, saith the LORD, thoughts of peace, and not of evil, to give you an expected end." I truly believe that God allowed me to go through my bullying experience to become the nurturing and caring teacher I aspired to be at the age of five. It made me the strong survivor that I am today. My experience also made me develop a greater love and passion for teaching early childhood and elementary school. I set out to be the best teacher that God called me to be by genuinely caring about them and being there for them when they needed someone to talk to. I never wanted to be a part of the problem; I wanted to be the solution to the problem. Whenever my students were not getting along with each other, I always implemented conflict resolution. This gave each student a chance to talk about the problem and reach a consensus to resolve it. I refused to be that teacher who ignored my students by "sweeping issues under the carpet." I made certain that we considered ourselves as a family in our classroom. The parents were also involved and updated often on their child's behavior and progress. My goal was to teach from the heart, respect each student's differences, and make an impact.

I stand firm on my core values of the word "FAITH."

MY CORE VALUES:
Follow Christ With A Passion
Always Love One Another
Increase In God's Word
Teach One Reach One
Have Compassion For Those In Need

If you have ever been bullied before, know that God allowed you to go through it to strengthen you into becoming the survivor you are today. Remember, God's plan is not ours. He works on a much greater platform, so trust His process!

"Being confident of this very thing, that he which hath begun a good work in you will perform it until the day of Christ Jesus."
Philippians 1:6 (KJV)

Brenda Sawyer

Brenda Sawyer is a native New Yorker who currently resides in Philadelphia. She has a strong spiritual foundation that acknowledges she is a Woman of God who believes that she can do all things through Christ who strengthens her. Brenda is a retired elementary school teacher who holds a second Master's Degree in Elementary Education from Cabrini College. Retirement allows Brenda to impart her knowledge through writing books, speaking engagements, and mentoring young women. Brenda is the author of Encouraging Words For The Mind, Spirit, And Soul, along with numerous book anthologies and collaborations. She is also the Founder and CEO of GIRLS WALKING WITH INTEGRITY EMPOWERING FOR DESTINY (GWWI), a Christian mentoring ministry which empowers young ladies between the ages of eight and eighteen to become transformed into all that God has called them to be.

You may connect with Brenda Sawyer at:
www.brendasencouragingwords.com
www.girlswalkingwithintegrity.com
www.facebook.com/brendasawyer.58
www.instagram.com/brendasawyerencourages

Looking for Love in ALL the Wrong Places

By Randi Scudder-Francis

When you look back over your life, you finally see how God has been with you all along, even when you did not know Him, even during the times you felt alone. He knows the plans that He has towards you. It is of good, not evil, to an expected end. Sometimes life takes you through some things that bring you to a halt and delays the place that God wanted you to be all along. That SECRET PLACE.

Twenty-five years ago, I had to do one of the hardest things in my life, something that would change the trajectory of me and daughters' lives forever. It has taken me years to write this down. But ladies, the only way for you to be free from your past is to empty what has been holding you back for the past 10, 20, or 30 years. Once you do, God will catapult you into your anointed place. Let me take you there.

Not again! Opening my eyes and seeing the barrel of a gun. My husband, the man I loved. The man I thought loved me. For the second time in our marriage, I am looking down the barrel of a gun. After the first time, I started sleeping with a knife under my pillow. Yes, ladies – IT WAS BAD!

You see, I did not even tell my Mom what was going on. I had a girlfriend who encouraged me to leave. I told her I couldn't. My second marriage, with two kids from two different daddies and unemployed. I told myself, "next time this happens, I'll just fight back?" He just kept pointing that gun, cussing me out. I do not even remember what he was saying. All I was thinking was that my life was over. Tears were rolling down my face. Do I continue living in fear, or do I want to take my life back? If I fight back, what will happen to my two daughters. What if he snaps and hurts them? Many of you may have been in this same situation. So, I just stared back at him, kept quiet, and finally, he walked away.

Then one morning, I got the courage to do it. My hands sweaty holding the phone receiver - ready to dial. (You were probably thinking I was holding the gun on him. But then I probably would not be writing this memoir today). I have dreamt about this moment over and over again. How do I call the police on my husband? The father of my second child. I do not know what was different on this day. I walked the gun down to the police station. Yes, ladies. I guess I was through. No, I was not thinking. They questioned me at the police station, and I told them what has been going on for the past two years. They asked if I wanted him arrested, and I said yes. They asked if I wanted a restraining order. At first, I hesitated, but then I said - yes. Not wanting to do it in front of the kids, I told the police to come before the kids got out of school. And to put a towel over the cuffs when they take him. You know how we do, ladies—not wanting everyone in our business. Even though I did not know God yet, He was there - protecting me.

Now let's talk, ladies. Some of us, not all, are looking for love in all the wrong places. Thinking a man can give you what you need—not even knowing or loving yourself. You look and see the world fornicating, living in sin. All the drinking, smoking, cussing. Ungodly living. It looks fun. It all looks normal cause everyone else is doing it as my Mom would say – that doesn't make it right. We served the devil well a time or two. As a teenager, you feel that you are not loved and that the world is against you. And your parents are from another planet; they just don't understand. And now, after being alive only 17 years, that you know more than your parents do. Yeah, I lived at home with both of my parents. But what it boiled down to was that I thought

I was missing something – REAL LOVE. And I started looking for love in ALL the wrong places.

Let's backtrack a little. As I told you, this was my second relationship. Me and my fast self, back in high school, I started getting a lot of attention from boys at the age of 13. I was involved in a lot of school activities: basketball, softball, track, music – but it still felt like something was missing. By the age of 17, I was pregnant. WHAT???!!! I had just come from a college where my current basketball coach would be coaching the next year, and I went to meet the team and tryout. And guess what? I made the team. They were even going to give me a scholarship. Well, I messed that up and had to turn it down.

I did not even tell my Mom. But by the second month, she pulled me aside and asked, "Is there something in the oven you want to tell me about?" First of all, what was she talking about? I looked at her and said, "I not cooking anything in the oven." My Mom looked at me with stern eyes and said, "are we going to have the little pitter-patter of feet running around here." Then I knew she knew. She asked me what we were going to do. I told her we don't know yet. She encouraged me to marry him – even though I was not in love with him. I loved him, but as we all know, there is a difference. We got married—the biggest mistake. Me and my fast self again, I almost died with a second pregnancy. The embryo was in one of my tubes - ectopic pregnancy. Doctors had to pump blood out of my stomach. They said if I had waited ten more minutes, I would have died. God gave me a second chance – even though I did not know Him yet. Grace and mercy. Of course, it didn't last, and we divorced less than two years later.

Then I met someone else, and I knew this was it. My Mom said – "girl, what are you doing? You need some time alone. There's nothing wrong being by yourself for a while." And I would tell her, "I'm grown, and I knew what I was doing. It's going to be different this time." She did not argue with me. I guess she said to herself, "she will have to learn the hard way." Hhmmm. Same thing I told my kids when they were younger.

This time, I waited a little while. I started talking to a guy, but I would not let him in my house right away because of my two girls. I made him wait a little - almost a year. We would meet in the hallway or talk in the staircase. He respected me, and he waited. This time, I fell in love. Still didn't do things in the right order, but I guess God gave me another chance to get it right, yet again. Six months after our son's birth, we got married and have been happily married for 24 years now. And no, it has not been perfect. We all have some things we need to work on. Yes, I am in love with my earthly husband, but it's still not the greatest love of all.

Not until I met Jesus. That is the GREATEST love you will ever know. I wish I would have met Him earlier. But I started looking for love in all the wrong places. But guess what, this type of love won't hurt you, cheat on you, or lie to you. This type of love is unconditional. The kind of love that hopes and endures all things. Whheeww! When God breathes His Spirit on you – EVERYTHING CHANGES!

Before you were formed in your mother's womb, He knew you. All the things you have gone through in life is for a reason and a purpose – HIS PURPOSE. You have come to the Kingdom for such a time as this. Just stay on the potter's wheel and let God mold and shape you into the woman He created you to be.

My Apostle's favorite saying is your misery will be your ministry. I now mentor and minister to young teen girls, teaching them biblical principles to apply in everyday life. Letting them know who they are and Whose they are – in Jesus' Name, AMEN!

TO BE CONTINUED….

Stay tuned for Chapter 2 of "Looking for Love in ALL the Wrong Places" – THE ENCOUNTER on my website. Coming Summer 2021.

Randi Scudder-Francis
Servant of God, Pastor, Wife, Mother, Business & Community Leader

Pastor Randi Scudder-Francis has been in ministry for over five years under the tutelage of Apostle H. Sheldon McCray in Greensboro, NC. Pastor Randi is V.P./Executive Director of the Nehemiah Community Empowerment Center. This non-profit's mission is to empower and enrich the lives of at-risk youth, teens, and adults in Guilford County. It focuses on exposing people in under-served communities to the STEM, robotics, and I.T. fields and creating jobs. Their mandate is to help decrease the educational inequity and financial and social disparities in society today.

Nehemiah's website is https://www.nehemiahcec-gso.org.

Pastor Randi is also the Founder and President of He Is Able Enterprises, LLC, to help start-up businesses get established. She teaches financial empowerment and stewardship workshops.

He Is Able Enterprises, LLC
"The Connection is DIVINE" – John 15:1-8
Entrepreneurial Training with a Spiritual Touch
https://www.hiaenterprises.com
randi@hiaenterprises.com

Standing Between Death and Determination
By Lindsey Vertner

It was pitch black, and I wasn't standing at all. Actually, I tried standing, but I couldn't even move. As my eyes adjusted to the darkness, I realized that I had no clue where I was. I went to call out, but I couldn't speak. I began to panic because I feared that I'd been tied up, kidnapped, and was being held in some psycho's basement. I mean, what other explanation could there be?! My tireless efforts to free myself only exhausted me to the point that I passed out.

The next morning, I woke up and thought to myself, "What an awful nightmare! It felt so real!" Unfortunately, I still couldn't see despite the sunlight, and I slowly realized that I still couldn't move, still couldn't talk, and still didn't know where I was. Before I could panic again, a lady walked up to me and began filling me in on what had occurred over the past week of my life.

On May 13, 2007, a "fatal" car wreck left me brain-dead and paralyzed. The car I was driving had flipped multiple times (as if it were doing backflips) before going off the opposite side of the highway and landing upside down in a ditch. After being cut out of the mangled car, I was pronounced brain-dead on the scene. I was flown by emergency helicopter to the nearest trauma hospital. Despite being pronounced brain-dead a second time, surgeons attempted to relieve pressure from my brain and piece my skull back together. After multiple surgeries, doctors still didn't expect me to make it through the night. However, God had other plans for my life because metaphorically... I WAS still standing!

Standing At The Crossroad

Imagine that one minute you're on your way home from visiting your mother for Mother's Day, and the next minute you're waking up being told you were brain-dead and paralyzed with no recollection of an entire week of your life. What would you do? For me, the only thing I could think of was, "Thank God I'm alive!" And physically, I was alive. However, mentally, it was still unclear if I would die inside as the result of a life I didn't ask for.

At that moment, I had a choice to become a victim to my circumstances or to become a victor over my obstacles. When we are in victim mode, we give up our power for change. In moments of adversity, a choice has to be made to stand in your power to change your circumstances. A choice has to be made to either continue sitting in defeat or to stand up and fight for the quality of life that you desire.

So, I chose to stand in my power. I chose to live at my fullest potential. I chose to create the quality of life that I knew was waiting for me if only I were to stand up and fight for it. I was determined by any means necessary! Due to this, I went from brain-dead and paralyzed to fully recovered. The journey towards my physical and emotional recoveries didn't come easy, though. I had to master my mindset and do the work to allow my pain to evolve into my purpose. I want to share three ways to master your mindset and stand in your power, just as I did.

Stand In Your Faith

The first way to stand in your power is by being faithful in your spirituality. This helps to manage your emotions because it decreases your stress and overwhelm during times of uncertainty. The variables surrounding my wreck were very uncertain. Doctors were telling my family that I may not be the same person IF I were to wake up. Doctors told me that I likely wouldn't return to college, and I may not walk again. Despite what the doctors said, I believed what God said. I believed that I was spared for a purpose, and my life was just getting started – which didn't include me being paralyzed!

Stand With Intention

With that said, I wanted to walk again. Period! The second way to stand in your power is to be intentional. I didn't want to be confined to a wheelchair for the rest of my life. I didn't want to wait for other people to feed me or to bathe me. I was already alive. So, my biggest goal became being able to walk again, and that's where I set my intentions. I didn't care about any of my diagnoses. (After all, the doctors were wrong before.) I knew what I wanted, and I was willing to do whatever it took to get it.

When we're intentional about what we want and don't want for our lives, it becomes easier to guide our actions. It becomes easier to overcome our obstacles because we know what we're working to achieve. And to be clear…setting intentions does not make it EASY; it makes it EASIER! It's easier to keep pushing when struggles arise because there WILL be obstacles along the way. There's no question about that. It's easy to give up when we don't know what we're fighting for, though. It's easy to lose sight of our goals when we remain in victim mode. Remember, there's no power in playing the victim because that means you're relying on external factors to change your pain. Also, fuzzy intentions create fuzzy results, and that's how we end up settling for less than we desire. So, be crystal clear.

Stand In Action

The third way to stand in your power is to be action-oriented. If we don't match our behavior to our thoughts, then nothing changes. We must take accountability for our actions (or lack thereof). When things aren't going our way, it's easy to point the finger at others. But that's playing victim to your circumstances. True change occurs when we recognize how we are contributing to our struggle or our success.

Because EVERYTHING we do (or don't do) moves us forward, back, or keeps us in the same place. It starts with setting our intentions and continues with actions.

For me, it wasn't enough to be clear and intentional about wanting to walk. I had to back up my thoughts with action. And guess what? It doesn't matter what anybody said or did; only I could make that choice to take action. How'd I do that? I went to therapy from 8 am to 6 pm, seven days a week, for weeks upon end.

Therapy was not fun by any means. It was more painful than not. But because I clearly set my intentions on what I wanted for my life; it was easier for me to continue to do the actions despite the moment's pain. I had to think about what pain I wanted to live with. Did I want the momentary pain of physical therapy and shock therapy for a few months? Or did I want the pain of being in a wheelchair and being dependent on someone else for the rest of my life? My family and my doctors couldn't do the therapy for me. I had to take action, and because I did, I was able to walk without a wheelchair, without a walker, and without a cane by the end of Summer 2007! So, ask yourself: would you rather live in the momentary pain of today or the lifelong pain of tomorrow? Then, take action accordingly.

Are You Determined to Stand In Your Power?

We all have the ability to choose whether we are a victim or victor over our struggles. Don't allow fear of the unknown and the pain of the present to dictate how you'll live your life. The pain from my wreck had a purpose that was bigger than me. During my recovery process, the things I learned led me to my purpose as a personal development coach and speaker. I can use my story to teach others how to master their mindset and overcome their obstacles so that they can live a life full of purpose, fulfillment, and happiness. I believe that if I can come back from death's bed, then there's no obstacle that you can't overcome to reach your dreams.

Never forget that you are more powerful than the blocks in your life. You are fully capable of achieving all that you desire. Don't let your current pain hold you hostage in victim mode. Remember to remain faithful, be intentional, and take action towards the life you desire! Don't let anything stop you from standing in your power and obtaining the victory that is waiting for you.

If you need guidance on taking action, download my free action plan guide at www.bit.ly/takeactiondownload. Also, I'd love to hear how you're standing in your power. Visit me at www.LindseyVertner.com or across all social media platforms by searching @LindseyVertner.

Lindsey Vertner

In 2007, a "fatal" car wreck left Lindsey Vertner brain-dead and paralyzed. Medical experts were amazed at Lindsey's miraculous recovery. She uses her unparalleled perspective to push her clients toward success in their personal and professional lives. Lindsey's expertise teaches female entrepreneurs and ambitious leaders how to master their mindset and increase their self-care, self-worth, and self-discipline (the "3 Pillars of Self").

As an award-winning peak potential strategist, transformational speaker, and multi-time Amazon #1 best-selling author, Lindsey's mission is to teach women around the world how to create their First Class Life™ full of purpose, fulfillment, and happiness. Lindsey is also the co-founder of The Unleashed Woman – a nonprofit organization that uplifts women of all backgrounds through empowerment and networking events. With a master's in Professional Counseling, Lindsey is a graduate of both Indiana and Liberty Universities. Connect with her at www.LindseyVertner.com and follow on Facebook/Instagram/YouTube by searching @LindseyVertner.

How To Find Your Sweet Spot, Passion, Purpose & Dream Job

By K. Venise Vinegar

Meditation For The Day:

SETTING AND ACHIEVING GOALS IS A LEARNED SKILL THAT WILL HELP YOU COMMIT TO THE FINISH LINE.

Do you have action plans in place designed to turn your dreams into a tangible reality?

Goal setting is a powerful practice you can use to achieve your dreams. The concept of S.M.A.R.T. goals helps you identify a clear start and end date. When goals are Specific, Measurable, Achievable, Realistic, and Time-bound, they become highly effective tools in helping you maintain focus and enhance motivation to continue working towards your long-term goals, even during hard times.

Daily Affirmation/Prayer: I free myself from the doubt and procrastination that keeps me from achieving my goals.

Greetings Everyone! I had been working in my dream job with The Walt Disney Company. After five years, I was blindsided with a letter of termination. My last day of employment would be August 14, 2011. In my exit interview, I turned over my picture I.D., my parking pass, and my free pass to Disneyland. Although I was laid off with 500 other employees, the sting of the blind side was immeasurable. The long walk of shame to my car was painful. I felt stripped of my identity, and very much alone. At age 57, I had lost my only source of income, doing what I loved. My expertise supporting corporate management and creative talent as an office management professional came to a screeching halt. I felt my career was over. However, the past nine years have been the most transformative and illuminating years of my life.

I had never aspired to work at a Fortune 500 studio. My training as a legal assistant opened that door in the 1980s. I loved being involved with the creative community that produced the television shows and films I had watched growing up. I was surrounded by individuals with high work ethics and who aimed for excellence. My first job was with David L. Wolper Productions, who produced "ROOTS." Paramount Pictures, 20th Century Fox, and DreamWorks followed, along with Indigo Productions -- working with comedian Richard Pryor and other amazing creative talent. My nights were spent at comedy showcases and actors' playhouses, scouting new talent as a casting assistant. My life was filled with excitement and adventure in a career that matched my personality. In 2006 Disney HR called with two career opportunities. I interviewed and landed the best match for me. Life was good -- until I received my termination letter five years later. The news was devastating.

My first week at home was difficult. I wondered how I could survive without a nine-to-five. I was able to continue to work with Disney as an independent contractor. I found joy in the flexibility of part-time work, combined with the freedom to focus on my personal and career development. My support groups kept me connected with community. LinkedIn Learning satiated my hunger for knowledge and discovery. Once again, I was doing something I loved, and I shared what I learned with others. I joined the non-profit organization Dress for Success as a client. They provided me with career counseling, interview outfits and became my anchor. In return, I became a long-time volunteer in the career center and a wardrobe stylist for other clients. I volunteered in the LinkedIn Lab, helping other women create their profiles.

Finding a passion for life-long learning and studying career development gave me a renewed sense of excitement and purpose. It kept my days structured and on point. In 2014, I turned my job search into an educational sabbatical. In 2017, I had gone as far as I could on my own trying to identify a new career path, but I still had not found the right job. I had a mini melt-down. I asked God for help and to show me a way to make a positive impact in the world. Then I experienced a Come to Jesus/surrender moment..

"Sometimes the simplest prayer has the power to help you transcend your suffering."

"Help is a prayer."

"When I use the word 'help,' I say, 'Hello, Eternal Loving Presence.'

That's what 'help' means to me."
Michael Bernard Beckwith

In answer to my prayer for 'help,' an extraordinary opportunity appeared to travel to South Africa with the AGAPE International Spiritual Center. The experiences I had there changed the trajectory of my life. Lisa Nichols, a global motivational speaker, was on that trip. I had no idea who she was. Lisa brought the house down as the keynote speaker at the Divine Feminine Conference in Johannesburg. I became an instant superfan. While attending that conference, I realized I had not fallen from grace when I lost my job with Disney; I had fallen *into* grace. I was given the power to imagine the unimaginable: *become the architect of my life and teach others how to do the same.* The Universe had answered my prayer.

Before I left for South Africa, I had been in the beginning stages of caregiving for my favorite aunt. She had taken care of me as an infant while both of my parents worked. Tragically, in January 2019, she suffered a traumatic brain hemorrhage. We went through hospice together, and she passed on the fourth day. I poured myself into completing the first draft of a book, I had begun to write which helped minimize my pain and grief.

Psalm 37:4 Take delight in the LORD, and he will give you the desires of your heart.

The Oprah Winfrey 2020 Vision Tour was the last event I attended before the Coronavirus lockdown. While quarantined, I was eager to develop a deeper state of spiritual consciousness. I also wanted to know how the rest of the world was coping. COVID-19 inspired me to expand my network globally and to include Mastermind Groups. That is when Dr. Cheryl L. Wood came into my life. She had the same effect on me that Lisa Nichols did. I was already on a mission to prove that at any stage in life and at any age, we have the power to become the beneficial presence on the planet we are meant to be. After six months of zoom meetings with Dr. Cheryl and a special zoom meeting that included Lisa Nichols, I was convinced that I could leave a footprint AND a legacy!

"If there's a book that you want to read, but it hasn't been written yet, then you must write it."
Toni Morrison

I took Toni Morrison's advice. My book idea, "Your Passion Is Your Purpose," is a work in progress. I am sharing tools I used to overcome adversity and carve out a new career *(in my 60s)*, that is my true calling. I have written and am now editing a 365-day devotional of thought-provoking questions, lessons, and affirmations. I intend to help others through my book(s) find their divine convergence of passion and talent to achieve prosperity.

"Your story is about you, but it is not for you"
Dr. Cheryl L. Wood

Helping others achieve their dreams is the thread that connects my past to my present. My journey has been the preparation to continue this work on a larger scale. Establishing core values helped me come up with a clear definition of success. That North Star pointed me towards my purposeful destination. Your passion for your talent will lead you to your dream job. When you chase purpose, the money will follow, and you will always be winning in life, love, and success.

If my story has inspired you to start your own journey – GET TO WORK! Below are the best practices, tips, and books that helped me find my sweet spot!

BEST PRACTICES

- Make a list of companies doing the work you like.
- Be sure a company brand and culture is a match for you.
- Use LinkedIn to nurture relationships that generate reciprocity.
- Grow your network. Make it diverse, spiritual, and global.
- Envision your ideal life. Write it down and pursue it with intention.
- Time is golden. Put up boundaries to protect it.
- Surround yourself with people who educate, elevate, and celebrate you!
- Live every moment and every day in an Attitude of Gratitude – no excuses.

5 JUICY TIPS!

1. Career Assessments reveal WHO you are.
2. Have the courage to follow your intuition and what brings you joy.
3. You have everything you need to undertake the role you are created to perform.

4. Your inner voice will reveal the answers that will help you discover your gifts.

5. Your sweet spot is what you love to do, excel at, and what people will pay you to do.

BOOKS:

- Lifevisioning
- What Color Is Your Parachute?
- Who Moved My Cheese?
- The 7 Habits of Highly Effective People
- Create Your Yes
- The Four Agreements
- The Career Fitness Program
- A Curious Mind – The Secret to a Bigger Life

Peace, Love and Blessings!

K. Venise Vinegar

"YOUR PASSION IS YOUR PURPOSE!" (First Edition)

* HOW TO FIND YOUR PASSION, PURPOSE AND DREAM JOB – EVEN DURING HARD TIMES!

* PERSONAL GROWTH! EDUCATION! SELF-HELP! 365-DAILY DEVOTIONAL

* CAREER DEVELOPMENT BEST PRACTICES, TIPS & SOLUTIONS TO TRANSFORM YOUR LIFE

* LAND BEST FIT CAREER OPPORTUNITIES AND DREAM JOBS THAT ARE A MATCH FOR YOU!

www.linkedin.com/in/venisevinegar

- In service to God to help uplift the lives of others locally and globally
- Editing 365-Day Devotional of Personal & Career Development Best Practices to show others how combining passion and talent equals prosperity. LOOKING FOR VC FUNDING!
- Vision Career Strategist for teens, young adults
- Holistic Declutter Specialist - Mind, Body & Spirit
- Time Management Guru
- End of Life Practitioner/Consultant
- Healthy Lifestyle Living Advocate
- Half-Marathon 17x Race Finisher

"IF THERE'S A BOOK THAT YOU WANT TO READ, BUT IT HASN'T BEEN WRITTEN YET, THEN YOU MUST WRITE IT"– TONI MORRISON

I Am Still Standing
By Crystal A. White

To be clear and certain, it is by the Grace of God that I Am Still Standing! As a young girl, I always felt different—not better —not lesser than anyone else—just different. That awareness caused me to always try to fit in. As I grew older, observed others, and learned from them, I realized that I would have to do things differently in my life to be all that I felt on the inside. Having older girlfriends caused my maturation process to speed up to the umpteenth degree. In that growing up scenario, I experienced a great many things that a child should not have to experience. I was molested around the age of six or seven. It could have been younger, but that's what I remember. I recall telling my mom as I cried about it on different occasions, and she did nothing. Resultingly, the abuse continued until I was about 12 when I realized the acts weren't normal and was old enough to say, "No" and "Stop."

At ten years old, on the 4th of July, I had my first menstrual cycle, was terrified, and did not understand what was happening to my body. When I got home, I told my mom while crying hysterically. She interpreted it as a rite of passage, phoned family and friends—telling them about my period's arrival. Intense anger accompanied these breaches of trust and triggered an internal decision to never confide in my mother again. Those initial bricks were the cornerstone of a wall I began building in my soul that would negatively impact and interfere with my ability to form productive relationships throughout most of my life.

My first pregnancy was at age 16. My mom's first reaction was taking me to her doctor and immediately scheduling the abortion. In my terrified state, mom's voice was loud and direct. She said, "You not having no babies for me to raise. Your life is ahead of you." At that moment, I felt like everyone knew what I had done and what I was going through. The feelings I was experiencing were hard for me to manage. They included shame, anger, sadness, hatred, and disappointment—landing me in a deep depression. It caused me to withdraw from friends, family, and my boyfriend and father of my never-to-be born child. Although a little older, my boyfriend and I were in high school, living with our parents, and unprepared to be parents. The entire ordeal was devastating to us both.

Going through the motions of life and trusting no one, I graduated high school in 1990. I was not financially prepared for college but knew I wanted to get out of my mom's house as soon as possible. As a first step in accomplishing that goal, I enrolled in Cosmetology School in DC Beauty Academy, renamed the Bennett Career Institute. Feeling like I was in the right place, I was focused and determined to make my life better despite all the obstacles I had endured as a child and teenager. Halfway through my completion of Cosmetology School, I was introduced to one of my classmate's cousins. That relationship escalated quickly with a lot of challenges, including being pregnant for the second time while still living with my mom. This time, things were different.

I had graduated high school, a legal adult, and almost finished Cosmetology School. Emotionally, I was having tragic memories regarding the first pregnancy. It took us about two months to tell my mom. I never will forget that day because I already knew what she was going to say. "Crystal, you got 30 days to find somewhere else to live because there's only one woman in my house, and that is me!" My son's father and I found an apartment in Northern Virginia; so, we moved in together. I felt like I was on top of the world, momentarily. I was out of my mom's house and had my own place with my soon to be child's father. Well, I was sadly mistaken. I spent many hours alone— not knowing my boyfriend's whereabouts or who he was with. I witnessed him coming home late each night, and at the time, that's all that mattered to me. I didn't want my family or friends in my business. I isolated myself from a lot of people that had become my safe place and coping mechanism. I would have some family visits but not many.

A short time after that, I completed Cosmetology School, had my beautiful son, and stayed home a few months with him. After that, I found a job doing hair as an assistant with a longtime family friend. As I thought things were getting better and before my son Andrew's first birthday, I had to sit in a DC courtroom while his dad was sentenced to 15 years imprisonment. My world was rocked once again. I sat there and cried, not knowing what I would do next. I wasn't prepared at all. I was being lied to through the whole process. Quickly, I had to regroup and make a new plan for my son and me. I had to put my pride aside and move back in with my mom temporarily, and that was truly crazy. From there, I stayed with one of my aunts, sleeping on her couch. My next pitstop was with the parents of an old friend from high school. During this nomadic existence, I found out I was pregnant again by my son's father prior to him going to prison. I said to myself, "This is too much for me to handle, and I want to give up." I was not about to have another baby to raise by myself. I remember being so broken and sad that I took a bottle of prescription pain pills. With my son at daycare and no one else home, I just laid there. I had written a letter to my mom and another for my son. I remember getting very scared and anxious.

I tore up the letters, got up, and walked to the Howard University Hospital near my mom's apartment on 5th & O Streets. Upon arriving at the ER, I told them what I had done in an unassuming soft voice. Quickly after the confession, I was in a room strapped to a hospital bed and shocked that I had been checked into the mental ward. It was a standard procedure for those attempting suicide. Upon drinking a charcoal substance, I vomited up all the pills I had taken. After what seemed like forever, my mom picked me up. She already had my son with her, and she said nothing the whole ride back to her place. I just held my son and cried. After aborting for the second time, I promised my remaining son, Drew, that I would never leave him or let anyone hurt him.

At that point, I decided to do something different for both of us. I started attending a Sunday night service with who I call my other mother. She was one of the people that took my son and me in earlier. As a result, I received the Lord Jesus Christ as my personal Savior—Amen, Hallelujah. My son and I were baptized together at a Revival at FREE Gospel Church. I was with some of my family, and one of my aunts introduced me to a man who became my husband eight months later. Even though I forewarned him of mostly all I had experienced, he still was interested in being with me. I said, "Okay, God, you are giving me another chance." Not recommending this to anyone, my soon to be husband and I met in January 1996 and married in August of that same year. I thought I had my knight in shining armor—a man sent by God. For a while, it appeared that way to me and many others. We opened, and I started my first Hair Salon. I miscarried our first child together, thinking I was being punished for what I had done earlier. It was devastating to us both. My doctor said, "Try again. It happens." In God's appointed time, we had our princess daughter Kayla. She was truly another gift from God. After attending Spirit of Faith for a couple of years, we pastored our own church, New Life Christian Center, for 17 years. Regrettably, after 22 years of marriage, I filed for divorce, and it was finalized in December 2017.

With all that I've been through, I Am Still Standing and moving forward in my purpose. The same is true for you. Be strong in your faith while awaiting your next chapter. Stand still and allow God to work in you so He can work through you.

Declaration: **I AM NOT WHAT I HAVE BEEN THROUGH. I AM WHO GOD CREATED ME TO BE!**

Crystal A. White

Crystal A. White has experienced the healing journey from despair to self-reliance that she passionately wants others to take. She is unapologetically transparent as she leads down the path of self-discovery, self-help self-empowerment, and self-love, as I am evolving into all God has created me to be and do in the Marketplace and The Kingdom of God.

About The Visionary, Dr. Cheryl Wood

Join Dr. Wood's community of entrepreneurial women:
www.Bit.ly/eesquad

Dr. Cheryl Wood is an international empowerment speaker, 11x best-selling author, leadership expert, and master speaker development coach for women. She equips women entrepreneurs with the tools to unleash the power of their voice, transform lives with their story, and monetize their expertise. Dr. Wood has trained countless women leaders & influencers across the United States and abroad in South Africa, India, France, United Kingdom, Canada, and the Bahamas. She empowers women entrepreneurs to get out of their comfort zone, take calculated risks, pursue their big dreams, and create a living legacy.

Dr. Wood has been featured on ABC, Radio One, Forbes Magazine, Huffington Post, ESSENCE, Black Enterprise, Good Morning Washington, Fox 5 News, Fox 45 News, The Washington Informer, The Baltimore Times, Afro-American Newspaper, and numerous other media outlets. She has delivered riveting keynote presentations for a host of large and small organizations including NASA, The United Nations, Verizon, The FBI, United States Department of Defense, United States Department of Agriculture, National Association of Legal Professionals, Federally Employed Women, Blacks In Government, Women's Council of Realtors, Women in eDiscovery, Women's Business Center of Charlotte, eWomenNetwork and the Congressional Black Caucus, to name a few.

FOLLOW ON SOCIAL MEDIA AT @CherylEmpowers
www.CherylEmpowers.com
www.Bit.ly/eesquad